THE

ST. MARY'S CO. P9-ARF-023 MARYLAND

ST. MARY'S CITY, MARYLAND 20686

Religion and Hopi
Life in the
Twentieth Century

Religion in North America
Catherine L. Albanese and Stephen J. Stein, editors

Religion and Hopi Life in the Twentieth Century

JOHN D. LOFTIN

INDIANA UNIVERSITY PRESS
Bloomington & Indianapolis

© 1991 by John D. Loftin
All rights reserved

No part of this book may be reproduced or utilized in any form or by
any means, electronic or mechanical, including photocopying and
recording, or by any information storage and retrieval system, without
permission in writing from the publisher. The Association of American
University Presses' Resolution on Permissions constitutes the only
exception to this prohibition.

The paper used in this publication meets the minimum requirements of
American National Standard for Information Sciences—Permanence
of Paper for Printed Library Materials, ANSI Z39.48-1984.

Manufactured in the United States of America

Library of Congress Cataloging-in-Publication Data

Loftin, John D., date.
   Religion and Hopi life in the twentieth century / John D. Loftin.
     p.   cm. — (Religion in North America)
   Includes bibliographical references and index.
   ISBN 0-253-33517-5 (alk. paper)
   1. Hopi Indians—Religion and mythology. 2. Hopi Indians—Social
life and customs. I. Title. II. Series.
E99.H7L64 1991
299'.784—dc20
                                             90-37968
                                               CIP

1 2 3 4 5 95 94 93 92 91

Contents

For Ang and Little John

Foreword

The publication of John D. Loftin's *Religion and Hopi Life in the Twentieth Century* provides an occasion for the Religion in North America series to realize a set of goals it has had since its inception. The series editors have wanted to integrate the study of small and marginal groups, including American Indians, into the comprehensive study of religious North Americana. They have wanted such study of the marginal to begin to question or even to dissolve the category of marginality. And they have wanted pursuit of the marginal to show its consequence for understanding aspects of the mainstream.

Given the ambitiousness of these aims, the series is fortunate that Loftin's fine work tackles a related agenda in its study of the Hopi. The first work on American Indian religion to appear in the series, Loftin's volume successfully joins the exposition of the "timeless time" of traditional Hopi religion with a reflection on the ephemeral time of the late twentieth century. On one hand, Loftin writes as a student of the comparative and phenomenological history of religions, elucidating classic features of Hopi religiosity that make it almost a textbook case of the fusion of sacred and ordinary. On the other hand, Loftin pushes past traditional exegesis to depict a present of fluid and uncertain direction. In so doing, he comes to terms with Hopi prophecies that, if discussed at all outside Hopiland, have been cited until now mostly by nonspecialists in popular and New Age journals. Thus readers learn in Loftin's study that the Hopi cope with the acids of American modernity by making sacred the very process of religious decline. Through belief that this decline was prophesied in the "long ago," Hopi people locate it in terms that continue to be religiously meaningful to them.

In exploring the practical dimensions of this prophetic stance,

Loftin's work is a model of a new kind of Native American study. Loftin has Hopi "consultants" instead of the ubiquitous anthropological "informants," and he goes to school under Hopi tutelage as a bright and sensitive non-Hopi student. The self-reports of his subjects, therefore, attain a stature that makes the examination of Hopi prophecies more than an exercise in pointing to the erosions of a dominant culture. Hopis emerge as equal partners in an unequal cultural exchange, as survivors who move creatively amid cultural assault and who change assault into the raw material of accommodation. Some readers might consider it merely trite to remind them, as Loftin does, that the Hopis are human as other Americans are human. Nonetheless, the reminder serves to flatten aspects of marginality, and it invites readers to see the mainstream itself from a different perspective.

Hence, *Religion and Hopi Life in the Twentieth Century* emerges as an engaged work. Methodologically quite different from other volumes that have appeared in this series, Loftin's study will, we hope, be read and discussed by Hopi specialists and more general readers, by those interested in Native American studies, and by those others who come to such studies from the point of view of the mainstream.

Catherine L. Albanese and Stephen J. Stein,
series editors

Acknowledgments

Though portions of this study come from my doctoral dissertation, "Emergency and Ecology: A Religio-Ecological Interpretation of the Hopi Way," it is a completely different work and not simply a revision of my thesis. I have relied on my thesis no more than any other source, and the material I have used from it has been greatly condensed.

This work differs from my thesis in several ways. First, I feel no need here, as I did there, to demonstrate a competence in Hopi studies. Second, I am much more concerned here with twentieth-century Hopis. In fact, most of the second part of this book was researched and written after I presented my dissertation to the Department of Religion at Duke University in 1983. It relies heavily on my field research conducted over six summers, from 1980 through 1985. This work also depends less on formal theory and method than did the dissertation. Theory and method are embodied in the text primarily as a means of illuminating Hopi religious experience and expression.

There is no way I can properly thank all of the people who contributed to the completion of this short book. Nonetheless, I feel compelled to extend my appreciation to some special persons who were involved in assisting me at various steps along the path to publication.

First, I thank my teacher, Charles H. Long, whose contribution to my intellectual development has been invaluable. Professor Long's lively religious instinct and far-ranging scholarship provided me with a climate in which my own work could germinate and grow to fruition. It is only fair that I credit my teacher with most of the worthwhile aspects of this study, while I, of course, accept full responsibility for its shortcomings.

I also want to single out the contribution of Fred R. Eggan, the "grand old man of anthropology," as he was once described by Emory Sekaquaptewa. Professor Eggan has worked among the Hopi as a friend and scholar for more than half a century, gathering insights into their way of life that are extraordinary and invaluable. For his patience in sharing his wisdom with me, I will always be grateful.

I also want to acknowledge the help I received from Emory Sekaquaptewa in spelling Hopi terms. There are about as many different ways to write Hopi as there are studies of the Hopi, and Sekaquaptewa is putting together a Hopi-English lexicon that will be of great benefit to scholars. The Hopi orthography developed by Sekaquaptewa is identical to that of Ekkehart Malotki (see the annotated bibliography), whose Hopi alphabet is considered standard. Because the popular spellings of Hopi village and proper names are so well known, I chose to use them in this book rather than the proper terms so as not to confuse readers who are already familiar with them. I have also decided to use the term *kachina* rather than the more proper *katsina*, again because the former term is so widely used.

For research grant monies that made my six trips to Hopi possible, I thank my late grandfather the Honorable John D. Larkins, Jr., and my late great-aunt Mary Lee Weikel. Also I thank my long-time friend Lester Ray.

For three of the last four summer sojourns to Hopi, I extend my appreciation to the Faculty Research and Development Committee at Elon College, which generously granted my funds four consecutive years. A scholar feels honored to gain the respect of his colleagues, and I am certainly no exception.

I would also like to thank Matthew Davis, a writer and editor who carefully read the text and made several helpful editorial criticisms and suggestions. Though it would be impossible to develop me into a great writer, this work is certainly better written now than it was originally, due to Mr. Davis's insights.

It is also essential that I thank Martha Whittinghill for her invaluable help in copyediting the draft that was accepted for publication. Mrs. Whittinghill, who once worked among the Eastern Band Cherokee as a nurse, helped smooth a lot of rough edges in the manuscript, and for that I owe a debt of gratitude.

For typing the final draft I thank Gail Owens, whose perseverance and attention to detail continue to amaze me. For typing virtually all preliminary drafts of the manuscripts I thank Carolyn McGill, who unselfishly gave of her time and energy at Elon College. Other secretaries at Elon College who contributed to the typing of this manuscript are Lillian Pollock and Jane Morton.

I thank Jim Pace, a professor at Elon College, for moral support and friendship. And without the help of two Orange High School teachers I would never have made it to college: Mary Susan Gattis and Gary Maske.

Special mention should be made of the influence and instruction I have received lifelong from my parents, Dalton and Emma Sue Loftin. My interests and instincts in religious studies have been germinated in large part by my father and mother, both of whom have helped me more than I can ever say.

Finally, my wife, Ang, has somehow through the years tolerated, supported, and even loved a rather strange fellow through some very difficult and trying times. Without her love and support this work would not have been possible. Furthermore, she has provided me with the greatest gift I have ever received, a child, now a mischievous seven-year-old boy who gives me joy even while unsettling me with his boundless and unbridled energy.

Introduction

The Hopi, a Native American people numbering some eleven thousand, live primarily in small villages in northeastern Arizona. Most of these villages are perched above a sea of sand on three jutting ridges of Black Mesa, called First, Second, and Third Mesas. These mesas are roughly oriented east to west, with First Mesa lying farthest east, Third Mesa farthest west. Most of my field research was done on Third Mesa, and consequently Third Mesa has become the usual focus of my discussion in this book. Hopi is a harsh land, semiarid with no nearby rivers. But it is also a beautiful and awe-inspiring land that occasions spirituality at every turn. Hopiland speaks of a life that is difficult yet precious.

It is usual in writing a book about relatively unknown people who are small in number to tell something about their background. That would seem to be a simple task. And yet major problems arise when the outsider attempts to tell the history of the Hopi. Certainly it can be said that the Hopi speak a Shoshonean dialect that is part of the Uto-Aztecan language family. They live on a reservation granted to them in 1882 by an executive order of the United States president Chester Arthur. While their reservation is located on traditional Hopi lands, it is only a small part of the area that the Hopi claimed before contact with Europeans. Furthermore, Hopiland continues to shrink owing to encroachment by the Navajo, an Athapaskan-speaking Native American tribe whose reservation surrounds the Hopi. The relationship of the Hopi with the Navajo is best described as a conflict of native cultures. The Navajo are a nomadic hunting, gathering, and herding people, while the Hopi are primarily farmers settled in some of the oldest continuously inhabited villages in the New World.

But where did the Hopi come from? Here Hopi and non-Hopi accounts vary. Most scholars in the Western tradition say that all

Native Americans migrated over land to the New World from Asia some time during the last Ice Age and that the Hopi migrated to their present home from the desert of what is now California some time between A.D. 500 and 700. The Hopi version is much different. The Hopi talk at times about migrations from the Old World to the New World, but they assert that the trip was made by raft across water, not on foot across land. And they talk even more about emerging to this world through the womb of the earth.

Moreover, the time frames of the Hopi are very different from those of Westerners. Whereas Westerners emphasize time, Hopis emphasize timelessness. Westerners see history; Hopis see myth. And myth is no illusion to the Hopi; indeed, it is reality, and reality is both spiritual and practical.

The Hopi Indians have been the subject of numerous scholarly and popular studies. David Laird compiled a bibliography of Hopi works in 1977 that included almost three thousand works, and many more have been published since then. And yet a comprehensive and systematic description and interpretation of Hopi religion has not yet been written, even though anthropologist Fred Eggan called for the gathering of much more knowledge of Hopi ceremonialism as long ago as 1950.[1]

The lack of a systematic study of Hopi religion stems in part from the fact that the Hopi have been investigated mostly by anthropologists, who have tended to interpret the Hopi religious orientation as it relates to social structure and material culture. That is to say, most studies of Hopi religion have dealt with social and material dimensions rather than with religion itself. True, Hopi religion is inseparably related to all other aspects of the Hopi orientation to the world, but it would be just as valid to study the religious dimension of Hopi social structure, material culture, and ceremonialism as to study the social structural and material cultural dimensions of Hopi religion. The literature, however, has all too often neglected the study of Hopi religion in its own terms.

Anyone familiar with the literature on Hopi religion knows implicitly that every significant aspect of Hopi existence embodies a religious dimension and meaning. Walter Hough made this point quite clearly, though abstractly, when he noted that "if we could pick the threads of religion from the warp and woof of Hopi life, there apparently would not be much left."[2] Peter Nuvamsa, a respected Hopi elder, made the same point even more succinctly when he stated that "everything that is Hopi is spiritual."[3] Similar statements fill the literature not only on the Hopi but also on other Native Americans, demonstrating, at a general level, a common understanding, however vague and abstract.

The problem becomes acute when one seeks to find studies that unravel the modalities through which the religious dimension is manifested. One soon learns that there is a serious need for an interpretive study of Hopi religion that deciphers the various modes of religious experience and expression. That is what this work attempts to do, insofar as it is possible to articulate the religious meanings embodied within the Hopi way of life.

The Sacred: *A'ni Himu*

Underlying and interconnecting the phenomena of Hopi experience is the sacred. The sacred—that is, basic reality—is known by several Hopi terms, though many of them are kept secret from the uninitiated. To best get at the Hopi view of ultimate reality, I will use the common term *a'ni himu*. The Hopi understand significant practical, social, and perceptual activities as experiences of *a'ni himu*.

Milo Kalectaca of Shongopavi, a village on Second Mesa, defined *a'ni* as "hard, well, strong, very" and *himu* as "something" (or "what" when used as a question).[4] Emory Sekaquaptewa, an interpreter of Hopi culture from Kikotsmovi, Third Mesa, told me that *a'ni himu* meant "very something." Both interpretations are close to that of linguist Edward Kennard, who defined *a'ni himu* as "Mighty Something."[5]

A'ni refers to the great power and autonomy of that which the Hopi experience as ultimate, and *himu* refers to the mysterious, ineffable character of that which the Hopi experience as ultimate. Religious experience among the Hopi involves their confrontation with "something" mysterious and incomprehensible. In that sense *a'ni himu* is not unlike William James's "something there" or Rudolf

Otto's "numinous."[6] Furthermore, the Hopi's own view of the sacred resembles that of other Native American people, such as the Sioux, Iroquois, Ojibway, Kwakiutl, Navajo, Crow, and Cherokee.[7]

Sekaquaptewa, who is coordinator of Indian Programs at the University of Arizona, told me that the term *a'ni himu* is purposely nonspecific, even being used to describe a number of significant secular phenomena. He said that the Hopi hold no specific definitions or concepts of the sacred, for they feel they cannot conceptualize that which created them. The sacred is experienced as constituting the very possibility of the world's existence, and thus the Hopi maintain that the sacred cannot be known in the strict sense. The Hopi feel they cannot grasp intellectually that which is their origin, sustenance, and end.

At the same time, the sacred does partially reveal itself through cosmic rhythms and forms.[8] To the Hopi, such rhythms and forms are powerful and autonomous, and Kennard also rendered *a'ni himu* as "that which is powerful but unknown"—that is to say, autonomous yet anonymous.[9] The experience of this ultimate power and mystery resonates throughout Hopi life. The cohesive quality of the sacred was made clear in 1951 by several ceremonial chiefs and elders from Shongopavi in a joint statement presented to the commissioner of Indian affairs: "Our land, our religion and our life are one."[10] While many non-Hopis have recognized the truth of this statement, until now no scholar has attempted a work that unravels the modes through which the Hopi law, the Hopi way of life, Hopiland, and the Hopi experience of the sacred are interrelated.

In addressing the Hopi religious orientation to the world, I have divided this book into two parts. Part I concentrates primarily on the traditional, mythic dimensions of Hopi religion, which are experienced as atemporal and eternal. The Hopi are viewed by and large—and not without cause—as a very conservative, slow-to-change people who have clung tenaciously to their law, their way of life, their land, and their religion for centuries, demonstrating at times an almost incredible degree of stability, comparable perhaps to the Old Kingdom in Egypt. I hope to show how the Hopi also manifest a timeless dimension in their religious orientation by reexperiencing the temporal era when the creation of the world took place.

Part II then reveals, however, that the traditional image of Hopi as static is incomplete. The Hopi disagree with the romantic notion that they are living fossils. They recognize historical changes, though most of these changes are simultaneously understood as taking place in mythic time. But the Hopi have also experienced another type of cultural change, which has not been so readily mythicized as atemporal and sacred. I refer to twentieth-century forced changes at the hands of the dominant European-American society. These changes have affected every aspect of the Hopi orientation to the world. Because I hope to show that Hopi religious experience now emanates from the paradoxical tension between myth and history, synchrony and diachrony, continuity and change, I have organized the whole book around this paradox.

More specifically, part I deals with the various modalities of the Hopi religious orientation to the world. Selected dimensions of all major aspects of the Hopi way are addressed—subsistence modes, kinship organization, rites of passage, basic perceptual experiences, the ceremonial calendar. The focus of the discussion of these phenomena is the relationship of work (*tumala*) and ritual (*wiimi*)—or, more broadly speaking, practice and religion, human activity and spiritual passivity.

I have often reflected on the relationship between these phenomena and have realized that the Hopi understanding is quite complex. Most white Americans link practicality with materiality and spirituality with imagination. They view work as an act in which people manipulate various material phenomena for practical benefits, as when a farmer plants seeds and harvests a field. Religion, on the other hand, concerns itself more with experiencing meaning in an imaginative way, which may have no practical value except to ensure a happy state of consciousness or perhaps an afterlife. But for the Hopi there is no such dichotomy between the practical and the religious. Their lives are lived in a continuum in which the practicality of an activity is seen in terms of its religious, not its material, dimension. Work itself is experienced as religious and therefore practical, while prayer is thought to yield material blessings, which are ultimately experienced religiously. Thus practice and religion are so interconnected in Hopi eyes that one cannot speak of one without the other. And this interconnection is apparent in two modes: the practicality of religious acts and the religious dimension of prayer blessings.

The first mode includes significant aspects of Hopi life, such as kinship classifications (clans and phratries), subsistence modes, rites of passage, and basic perceptual processes. When asked why they act in and perceive the world as they do, Hopis almost always say they have always done so, meaning that such practices were established by the ancestors in mythic times. All these practical activities are experienced as ultimate as transcending time and space—in other words, as sacred. It is precisely because of their sacredness that they are also perceived as practical, for the sacred gave birth to the world.

The second mode is concerned with the Hopi ceremonial calendar and more generally with the multitude of Hopi prayer rites. The literature on Hopi ceremonialism is extensive and need not be repeated here, especially since many ceremonies are no longer performed on Third Mesa, at least not in their full form. Therefore I limit my discussion to a detailed description and interpretation of Powamuya, a major winter rite still practiced on all three Hopi mesas. Powamuya includes almost every type of Hopi prayer rite and thus is a good example of the second mode of relationship between practice and religion. Powamuya, like other formal ceremonies and prayer rites, embodies the transcendence of time and space through the practical benefits gained by prayer. Asked why they pray, the Hopi almost always respond that they do so for rain, crops, health, and long life. Thus prayer is perceived as quite practical and efficacious. Prayer creates life, and life evokes experience of the sacred. I conclude part I with some general summary remarks about the relationship between practice and religion among the Hopi.

While part I is concerned primarily with traditional Hopi religious experience and expression, part II is devoted to twentieth-century Hopi history and cultural change. I purposely created a break within the book to portray more faithfully Hopi religious experience: there is now a gap in Hopi experience that will not go away. The Hopi of the twentieth century feel a painful tension between their traditional religious teachings and practices and the industrialized Western world. The Hopi experience that world in a qualitatively unique way that brings to play unprecedented cultural strategies and programs.

After a brief theoretical introduction to Hopi cultural and religious change, I examine some significant late nineteenth and twentieth-century events in order to unfold their implications for religion. My thesis here is in essence similar to the thesis of the entire work, although it is placed within a somewhat different and more limited context. On the most general level of experience, I believe, the Hopi feel a tension between their traditional, mythical religious orientation and the profound historical change that the twentieth century has brought. And yet within the context of twentieth-century cultural contact and change, the experience of the Hopi is paradoxical owing to their perception of history as unprecedented yet prophesied since the beginning. If the Hopi on one level experience the paradox of eternal myth and historical change, they also experience historical and cultural change itself with ambivalence. On one hand, it is viewed with regret and sorrow; on the other hand, the change itself is understood to fulfill the destiny of the Hopi way.

The Hopi have undergone unprecedented cultural changes as a result of their confrontation with the dominant society. In one sense their subjection to change seems meaningless and unfortunate. Yet a number of their prophecies (*navoti*) see the loss of their traditions as religiously significant, foretelling the demise of many customs just before the end of what the Hopi call the fourth world, the world we live in now. Such losses are said to mark the increasing corruption of Hopi spiritual values, which will eventually result in the purification of the world, so that life will begin anew and pure, fresh from the "giver of the breath of life." Peter Whiteley, in a book on the Third Mesa village of Oraibi, demonstrated that the loss of the ceremonial calendar was planned in the early part of this century, fulfilling ancient prophecies of an end of ceremonialism due to spiritual impurity and loss.[11] Thus the demise of the ceremonial calendar at Oraibi is understood as fulfilling the meanings and values of the Hopi way.

Hopi prophecy embodies a timeless dimension not unlike myth, and this atemporality also reveals itself in two modes. First, Hopi prophecies are experienced as having existed since the beginning so that, for example, the Hopi say that prophecies about the arrival and dominance of white people have always existed. Second, the Hopi say that such prophesied events have occurred before in a previous world and thus are not unique. Therefore there is an inseparable relationship between myth and prophecy. Indeed, it is difficult to distinguish between them, for both interpret what appear to be historically unique events in timeless and sacred categories. If there is a difference it is one of emphasis. Myth incorporates history into timelessness by forgetting the distinctive characteristics of events, while prophecy remembers the timeless dimension of events that are at first glance irreversible and historical. In any case, prophecy is the process through which apparently unprecedented dimensions of twentieth-century history are experienced as eternal and sacred. Prophecy thus embodies a paradoxical understanding of the twentieth century in which the Hopi experience a timeless spirituality within a mode of existence that faces forced change at every turn. The Hopi are hurt by the forced and rapid decline of the traditional Hopi way, yet such loss is viewed as fulfilling prophecies expressed since the emergence of the Hopi to this world.

Furthermore, it is important to note that Hopi eyes do not see all cultural change the same way. The Hopi recognize the European-American culture as dominant and, like other Pueblo Indians, compartmentalize a number of cultural patterns borrowed from that culture.[12] In other words, the Hopi sometimes change in order to remain the same. They recognize the political and military superiority of the United States and realize that they must observe certain rules and regulations imposed by the federal government. At the same time, many of these changes are accepted at a political level in order to preserve, as much as possible, more fundamental religious values and practices. The Hopi recognize, for example, the necessity of capitalistic wage earning to foster economic self-determination and thereby to maintain much of their traditional land, to which their religion is indissolubly linked. Or traditional religious values are themselves located in apparent cultural changes, such as the establishment of the Hopi written constitution. The Hopi recognize the inevitability of writing a constitution to deal effectively with the federal government. The Hopi constitution, insofar as it reflects Hopi input, attempts to embody traditional customs and values.

Also in part II I examine recent events that raise the question of whether or not the Hopi at times consciously and willingly violate the Hopi law of life in a manner that cannot simply be linked to the dominant society. Additions to Hopi culture, such as some medical techniques, are viewed as good and pose no real problem for Hopi religiosity. Indeed, many prophecies say that the Hopi must carefully select the good from the bad in all that is offered by whites. Some changes among the Hopi are clearly negative, however, such as overgrazing the earth for excessive short-term profits. But even such internal negative changes do not simply signal the inevitable end of authentic Hopi spirituality, for at least two reasons. First, losses and degradations of Hopi religious traditions are experienced with sorrow and regret, so that at least some memory of the custom is preserved. Second, losses and degradations are understood as manifestations of constitutive Hopi frailties and shortcomings, summed up in the Hopi axiom that all humans are clowns. The Hopi emerged in the beginning as clowns, and a sacred, atemporal dimension surrounds their very finitude and mortality.

Part II concludes with a theoretical summary examining the Hopi emergence myth as a structure expressing the paradoxical separation from and connection with the sacred that exemplifies the religious orientation of the Hopi to their world.

Part I

Work and Ritual

One

A Religious Practicality

It is commonly said that the Hopi are an extremely practical people who use every possible tool to survive in their inhospitable semiarid environment. Common also is the idea that the Hopi are extraordinarily spiritual, since much of their time is devoted to ritual activities. Both perspectives are true: the Hopi are very practical and very ceremonious.

The Hopi do not understand work as a secular activity that is somehow distinct from their religious life. Nor do they relegate religious matters to a few days a week, holidays, and major life events such as birth, marriage, and death. For them, work and ritual, practice and religion, are inseparably related.

Important activities of all kinds embody religious meaning for the Hopi. When Hopis weave cotton, they are not simply performing a technical act. Certainly they are doing that, weaving a piece of cloth. But they are also experiencing the sacred. By repeating the techniques laid down by a deity, Spider Woman, in mythic time, Hopis reexperience that timeless era and feel a sense of unity with their mythical ancestors. The practical act of weaving occasions experiences of eternity and relationship with the cosmos.[1]

But not only does practice evoke religious experience; religious experience is also practical. Indeed, religiously experienced activities are practical for the Hopi on two different but related planes, the existential and the cosmic.[2] On the existential level, the return to the mythic times ensures success in one's activities, such as weaving. For it was then, in that time, that Spider Woman first instructed the Hopi in the art of weaving. Hopi tradition holds that Spider Woman (Kookyangwwuuti) taught the Hopi how to weave

3

cotton in the "ancient time ago."[3] Spider Woman was the first to weave. Her techniques and patterns have stood the test of time— or, more properly, the test of timelessness—because they have always been present. It makes sense that one would follow the instructions of a deity who helped form the world in which one lives. The practical nature of a Hopi weaver's work is not experienced primarily as the result of one's own efforts but rather as a manifestation of the creative power of the gods. Weaving is not an act in which one creates something oneself; it is an act in which one uncovers a pattern that was already there.

Weaving is also practical at the cosmic level. It is an act that recalls the emergence of the Hopi from the underground to this fourth world through the earth navel *(sipaapuni)* in the "long ago."[4] To recall that era through the timelessness of weaving is to regenerate the world. For in the beginning all was fresh and pure, unspoiled by the passage of time. The reactualization of that epoch is practical, for what could be more practical than cosmogony? In this context one better understands the comment of Walter O'Kane, a sensitive observer of the Hopi, that the Hopi way of life makes "no formal distinction between practical affairs and those of the spirit because the two are indissolubly related."[5]

Hopi Farming

Emory Sekaquaptewa, a Hopi scholar who has been a ceremonial participant in rites in the Third Mesa village of Kikotsmovi, once told me that work in and of itself is significant for the Hopi because it symbolizes their emergence to humanity. The Hopi cosmogony holds that when the Hopi lived underground they were incomplete creatures, undergoing several phases of metamorphosis or gestation before finally emerging as fully human beings.

Just before their emergence, the Hopi and other peoples were given their pick of subsistence activities. The Hopi chose an ear of corn and became farmers. But they did not pick at random; they chose short blue corn to symbolize their choice of a life of hardship and humility. Hopi blue corn requires more work for a successful harvest than do other types, but blue corn is the strongest and most durable strain.

The symbolism of the blue corn runs throughout the Hopi religious orientation. Moreover, Sekaquaptewa told me that blue corn is the "Hopi law." Hopi life embodies the law of the short blue corn so that traditional Hopi activities are perceived as difficult but rewarding. As the Hopi often say, "it is hard to be a Hopi but good to be a Hopi." Indeed, it is the fear that life will become too easy that often motivates the Hopi to resist the benefits of Western technology. Hard work embodies the spiritual essence of the Hopi way, chosen in the primordium by their ancestors. By working, the Hopi feel a strong sense of identity with their mythic forefathers, who lived in the time before there was time. Working evokes the experience of the sacred, for it recalls—or, more accurately, reactualizes—the timeless time when everything was one with the sacred. Paradoxically, by working, by doing specifically human activity, the Hopi reexperience the creation of their world. For the Hopi, hard work itself affords the experience of the "very something," the *a'ni himu*, that constitutes their cosmos. Some traditional work patterns are perceived as more significant than others, but all evoke the experience of the beginning and hence are sacred by virtue of transcending time and space.

Hopi farming techniques, along with hunting, gathering, building, eating, and sexual activity, are among the most religiously significant activities performed by Hopis. The religious experience of farming is related to the religious dimension of Hopi kinship structures and the fundamental perceptions of their world. Because the Hopi traditionally have been vegetarians, subsisting mostly on the harvest of corn,[6] one might think that farming is simply a practical, economic activity for the Hopi, as it is for Westerners. Farming is unquestionably of economic importance for the Hopi, but that is because it is religious. The Hopi feel that when they farm as their ancestors did they become identified with their earliest predecessors, for Hopi farming techniques were first established by the god Maasaw when the Hopi emerged to the fourth world, and the Hopi feel that they return to that timeless era whenever they farm. Their experience of the emergence is practical, for it was then that proper farming techniques were taught by Maasaw.[7] Moreover, their return to the time before there was time renews the world, a religious experience of no small practical importance.

Hopi farmers clear their fields near the end of winter, usually in February, by trampling down or removing weeds and brush by hand or hoe, or more recently with a horsedrawn or tractor-drawn cultivator.[8] The ground is then broken with a *wiikya*, a stick about three feet long with a rather broad, sharp end, which is used with a paddlelike motion to cut the ground.[9] The field is then considered ready for planting, and the Hopi wait for their designated "sun watcher" to call out the appropriate times to plant various cultigens. Mischa Titiev, who conducted extensive fieldwork among the Hopi in the 1930s, found that twelve planting times were traditionally recognized at Oraibi village, and each corresponded to a particular topographical point in the distant horizon above which the sun appeared to rise.[10] By calling out the appropriate times for planting crops as well as for ceremonies, the sun watcher and the villagers experience transcendence of time, for they feel they have reactualized the eternal era, when crops were first planted. There is, of course, a practical dimension to Hopi planting times, but the Hopi rarely say that they plant according to custom in order to maximize the short growing season. Rather, they say they are planting as their ancestors did when they first emerged during the birth of the fourth world. In so doing they prevent frost damage, but not according to some scientific forecast. They plant as they were taught to plant by the gods who own the plants.

Traditionally—that is, before the twentieth century—the Hopi often planted their fields in working parties consisting of clan members.[11] By working together in the fields the Hopi reexperienced the settlement of the mesas by the various clans. Hopi tradition holds that as each clan was accepted into the tribe it was given clan land to farm together.[12] Furthermore, this experience has a practical dimension, for in mythic times the fecundity of the sacred was everywhere manifest, so that life and health were evident among all cosmic forms and rhythms.

Planting is done between the clumps of the previous season's plant stalks which serve as guides for the new plants.[13] Following the pattern of his ancestors, the planter crouches on one knee, swings the planting stick over his head, and digs a narrow trough twelve to sixteen inches deep, pulling the loose dirt toward him. The soil at the bottom of the hole is further loosened, and ten to twenty seeds are dropped in and covered with earth, the surface being packed down with hands and feet.

The digging stick, or *sooya*, holds great religious significance for the Hopi. According to Hopi tradition related to me by Sekaquaptewa, the *sooya* was given to the Hopi along with blue corn before their emergence to this world. It too symbolizes the life of humility and hardship chosen by the Hopi in the underworld in the "ancient time ago." To work with the *sooya* is to participate in the way of the "people of the long ago." Such repetition yields the experience of timelessness and its concomitant practical dimensions of fertility and creation.

Ernest Beaglehole, who studied the Hopi in the 1930s, noted that deep planting allows the seeds to receive the essential moisture they require from the ground and to develop a strong root system that helps the plant withstand the region's southwesterlies.[14] Planting several seeds produces several closely knit stalks that serve as protection from mice, worms, and southwesterlies. By harvest time only a few of the stalks generally remain standing; the others are eaten by wind and rodents. Yet, although the Hopi are aware of these facts, they do not emphasize the practicality of their planting techniques in those terms. The Hopi say they plant the way they do because that was the way of the ancestors, who learned their techniques from the gods. Since the gods created the world and taught the ancestors how to live, the Hopi strive to repeat ancestral patterns.

Their religious understanding of planting patterns can be further detected in the Hopi understanding of seeds. Seeds are not themselves responsible for the growth of plants. Rather, seeds tell Muy'ingwa, the underworld god or manifestation of germination, which kind of plant is desired. If the seed is planted by a Hopi with proper thoughts of humility and harmony, Muy'ingwa shaves or shakes the desired plant from his body and pushes it up through the soil.[15]

This belief does not contradict the widespread theory that Hopi agricultural methods are in fact ecologically sound in terms of generating a life-yielding harvest without exhausting the available natural resources. R. Maitland Bradfield, in conjunction with the Hopi Harry Masai'yamtiwa, demonstrated nicely the ecological viability of Hopi agricultural techniques.[16] The Hopi homeland of Black Mesa is a diamond-shaped plateau, sixty miles wide and six to seven thousand feet above sea level, that is dissected by the southwestward-flowing ephemeral streams of four washes. These streams carry sand and silt from Black Mesa to the valley floor below, where the prevailing southwesterly winds carry the sand back northward to bank it against the escarpments. Because of these alluvial fans, Hopiland has more permanent springs and less arroyo cutting than areas of similar climate nearby. This natural phenomenon helps explain how the Hopi could for many centuries maintain a somewhat sedentary agricultural orientation despite the paucity of annual rainfall. Rainfall in the valley below the mesas generally amounts to only ten to thirteen inches a year, so the permanent springs are vital for agriculture. Furthermore, Hopi corn requires 120 days to mature, and the growing season between frosts is about 130 days. The proper timing for planting corn and other cultigens is thus essential to the success of a fruitful harvest. Since the Hopi are dry farmers, they make every effort to conserve the water that rushes down to the valley from the mesas during spring thaws. The floodwaters are directed toward the fields by small ditches. Afterward the Hopi keep the fields clear of weeds, which would soak up the precious groundwater on which the crops depend.

The practical, ecological value of Hopi agriculture is obvious. But if asked why he farms as he does, a Hopi will typically respond, "because the ancestors did so," meaning "because the reexperiencing of the creation of the world is practically significant." The Hopi know that their farming techniques are life supporting, for they came into being during the creation of the cosmos. To farm as their ancestors did is to reactualize the fertility and fecundity of the sacred as revealed in the very formation of the world itself. Harmony with the environment is also ensured by Hopi farming techniques because of the practical value of following god-given instructions. In other words, the practical nature of growing crops and of other Hopi activities is ensured because it is religious.

Sekaquaptewa has noted that Hopis and other Native Americans are often perceived by European-Americans as symbols of conservation, but he is quick to add that Indians do not explain their sense of harmony with the environment in scientific terms.[17] He thinks it is fine for Native Americans to be viewed as living harmoniously with their world but wants to make it clear that Native Americans understand their relationship with the earth differently from Western ecologists. Richard Hart, in discussing the Zuni (the Hopi's closest Pueblo neighbors, both geographically and experientially), aptly remarked that the Zuni practice "conservation from the point of view of caring for a relative and not from a scientific point of view of conserving a natural resource"—a vital point.[18] Like the Zuni the Hopi perceive the earth as their mother, the one from whom they were born and receive their sustenance, and to whom they will return after death.

For many years the Hopi resisted the use of steel plows to prepare their fields for planting, and soil conservationists Guy Stewart and Ernest Nicholson stated that they did so because of the wind erosion that results from excessive soil disturbance.[19] The Hopi probably did notice that strong winds easily remove loose topsoil, but the primary reason Hopis give for not using plows is that such usage violates their primordial perceptions of the earth as their mother. The Hopi feel that a steel plow unnecessarily and cruelly tears the skin of the earth mother. Therefore Hopis plant their crops by digging narrow trenches with a digging stick usually made of greasewood, a child of the earth. The Hopi Don Talayesva insisted in his autobiography that digging sticks should be made of greasewood rather than metal, for metal sticks, like plows, hurt the ground.[20]

Hopis were taught by Maasaw how to revere the earth as a relative, and such reverence is necessary to reactualize the time of the emergence. The perception of the earth as a relative is essential for the Hopi to produce a life-yielding harvest. To treat the earth without respect is to neglect the feelings of humility and harmony that the ancestors chose in the beginning when they selected the short blue corn. Proper thoughts and feelings are, according to Hopi experience, necessary for fruitful communication with the sacred—a point that will emerge later in my discussion of Hopi prayer. Hopi tradition holds, futhermore, that Maasaw, the complex deity who owns the Hopi's land, agreed in the "long ago," after the emergence, to let the Hopi live on his land if they did so humbly and with good and harmonious hearts.[21] If the Hopi manifest arrogant, greedy, or disrespectful behavior, the gods may withhold the rains that are part and parcel of creation itself.

Barre Toelken, a Native American scholar, once asked a Hopi whether kicking the ground would bring about a poor crop harvest, to which the Hopi replied, "Well, I don't know whether that would happen or not, but it would just really show what kind of person you are."[22] This statement is typical of Hopi religious perceptions. Clearly the Hopi revere the earth in a manner that cannot be reduced to economic concerns.

Not that the Hopi have no awareness of practicalities. Peter Whiteley told me that when the Hopi plant corn they dig until they find sand wet enough to yield a drop of water when squeezed. Indeed, he said there is a Hopi term that describes such sand as "wet like a dog's nose," from which a drop of water can also be squeezed. The Hopi are aware, then, that plants need water. This point is further demonstrated by the great care Hopis take in clearing their fields of weeds, which suck precious moisture from the soil. It seems to me, however, that most Hopis perceive no fundamental tension between these practical insights and their religious understanding of the world. Moisture is perceived as not only necessary for plant life but also as the sacred essence of the cosmos upon which everything depends for life and sustenance. It is precisely because water is so important practically that it is understood more fundamentally as sacred. The Hopi make great efforts to preserve water, but they recognize that they do not create it; rather, water creates them. If there were no water they could not preserve it in order to farm fruitfully.

In addition, because water is associated with the spiritual substance of the world, it is not perceived as a finite resource. The sacred brings forth moisture according to its own intentions and purposes. Water can be given and it can be withdrawn by the "very something" that creates and sustains all life. The Hopi think of water not merely as a material phenomenon subject to unchanging and determined physical processes. Water is the essence of the sacred and can appear at any time. A shortage of moisture at Hopi is not the result of overuse in a scientific sense. Rather, it is the consequence of improper spirituality, which shows up in irreverent—that is, ignorant or greedy—interactions with the earth mother. Such improprieties violate the original covenant with Maasaw.

Maasaw not only gave the Hopi conditional stewardship of the land but also taught them about farming, fire making, wild game, and house building.[23] As the original ruler of the earth and a principal owner of Hopi crops, Maasaw would rush upon the farmers who had just finished piling up the freshly harvested corn in heaps. Attired in an old woman's dress put on backwards and with a mask of rabbit skin covered with fresh blood, Maasaw would chase the farmers, threatening to strike them with his club. The Hopi men would flee in terror, for Maasaw is also the god of death; to be struck by his club is to die. As the nineteenth-century Hopi scholar Alexander Stephen first noted, "Masau is death."[24] After chasing farmers for a while, Maasaw would go over to the corn piles and pat them with his hands. His actions reaffirmed his ultimate ownership of the Hopi's land; they also were understood as a blessing of fertility, for which he was thanked.

It may seem strange that a god of death—or rather the god who is death—would render a blessing of fertility, but Maasaw, after all, owns the Hopi land and taught the Hopi how to grow crops in the beginning. Maasaw may be death, but according to Hopi perceptions life comes from death. The spiritual source of all life and forms issues from the land of the dead, the underworld, where it appears as life-giving water. Indeed, the Hopi petition their own departed ancestors to visit their villages in the form of clouds to bless them with the sacred gift of rain. Thus death is understood by the Hopi as a return to the spiritual realm from which comes more life.[25]

The Hopi do not consciously conserve natural resources; they perceive no nature apart from themselves. The earth is their origin, nature, and destiny, and they do not perceive themselves apart from the world in which they live.[26]

Hopis and White Ecology

Whether or not Hopi farming practices have implications for Western civilization today is a popular area of speculation. The scholar Joseph Brown has lamented Western peoples' "de-traditionalization or despiritualization," which he thinks can be helped by a fruitful dialogue with Native Americans. Brown noted that Western peoples have come to question the very premises of their "materially dominant world" and suggested that Westerners might renew their own spiritual roots by understanding Native American religions.[27]

A more radical position was taken by the Sioux Vine Deloria, Jr., in his younger years. He said that nonnative European-Americans needed to shun their Christian roots and learn from the religious traditions of Native Americans. He argued that Indian tribal religions were necessitated by today's ecological problems and insisted that "for the white man even to exist, he must adopt a total Indian way of life."[28] Many others, including Thomas Overholt, have also perceived Native Americans as "natural ecologists" and have asserted that Westerners can learn much valuable information from them. Overholt, unlike Deloria, said that Westerners needed to draw upon the underlying values of Native American religions rather than borrowing their specific cultural patterns.[29]

To better understand the context of this movement, we need to reflect a moment on some remarks made by Emory Sekaquaptewa:

I think that what is happening here is that the white man's technological methods of controlling the environment have begun to produce results which have become a measure of the quality of life. It is really the white man's own question about the quality of his life which leads him to search for potential alternatives in the Indian way of life.[30]

What he is suggesting is that white people may not be able to find solutions to their ecological problems through an investigation of Native Americans because Native Americans do not share their problems. Whites created the problems, and they must find their own answers.

Indeed, one must ask whether it is unfair and exploitative to look to Native Americans to solve whites' problems. The Hopi and other Native Americans may perceive no nature apart from themselves, but they are not one with nature. According to Charles Long, a historian of religion, all human beings demonstrate "a mode of being which is continuous with nature on one level and discontinuous on another level."[31] The Hopi are neither animals nor spirits; they are humans and should be understood as such. That sentiment has also been expressed by Armin Geertz, a scholar of Hopi religion, who is quite critical of contemporary Westerners' attempts to come to terms with their identity crises through the projection of their problems onto the Hopi.[32] And not long ago I heard a similar critique from a Hopi, who said he resented being romanticized as noble and pure when in reality he and other Hopis are human beings with many problems of their own.

Two

A Sacred Society

The Hopi social structure closely reflects the Hopi perception of the world. Both embody a religious dimension that forms the thread holding these apparently disparate phenomena together. Hopi religious experience and expression constitute a fundamental and irreducible aspect of the Hopi way of life whose meaning and function in part are to bind and bond all planes of Hopi experience into a lived totality.

The Hopi experience the sacred by and through the profane material forms and rhythms of their cosmos. Mircea Eliade's remark that "nature is never purely 'natural' " rings true in Hopi perception.[1] Alfonso Ortiz, a Pueblo Indian, echoed Eliade's statement when he noted that the Pueblos—including the Hopi—think that all reality has "matter and essence," a material and a spiritual dimension.[2] For the Hopi, the spiritual and material planes of being presuppose each other, so that each is necessary for the other and neither is reducible to the other. In Hopi experience the spiritual and material dimensions always constitute a paradoxical totality.

The Hopi refer to the sacred as *a'ni himu* ("very something") or by various other terms, such as "giver of the breath of life" or "he who walks unseen."[3] The link between the sacred and breath is especially instructive here, for Kennard argued that *a'ni himu* and *hikwsi* are essentially synonymous terms.[4] *Hikwsi* refers to the Hopi soul or breath, which is said to live forever after the body dies. *Hikwsi* is thus the "spark" of deity which each Hopi embodies and which returns to the sacred ("giver of the breath of life") after death. Breath, moisture, cloud, and fog have all been referred to by the Hopi in describing the spiritual essence of the universe.[5] Moisture, or rather a certain aspect of moisture, is perceived by the Hopi as the "spiritual substance" of the cosmos and receives a name kept secret from the uninitiated. In fact, a primary purpose of the initiation of all Hopi youths into the Kachina cult is to inform them that the "spiritual substance" is their origin, nature, and destiny.[6] That the cosmos was created and is sustained by the "spiritual substance" is common knowledge among adult Hopis, a position perhaps best revealed by their emergence mythology.

The experience of the world as spiritual is not deduced logically by the Hopi; nor is it derived from an unverifiable faith. Their perception of the world is a result of their experience of the sacred. I have treated this matter more fully elsewhere, so a brief examination of Hopi deities will serve as illustration here.[7] As I noted in the first chapter, it is commonly said that Maasaw is, among other things, the Hopi god of death. Nonetheless, it would be a mistake (at least among Hopi elders) to consider Maasaw solely as a personal deity who metes out death periodically. Maasaw appears wherever and whenever death appears; to perceive death is to perceive Maasaw. The same kind of relationship between cosmic event and deity hold for the other Hopi deities as well, and thus it is fair to Hopi experience to say that all Hopi deities should be understood as so many refractions of *a'ni himu*, "very something."[8] The Hopi are not polytheistic; rather, they worship one spiritual substance that manifests itself in many modes of being.

The Hopi thus hold that the spiritual and material dimensions form an indissoluble relationship. The material world reveals the spiritual plane, and the spiritual plane undergirds and sustains the material world. We will see these relationships more concretely in looking at Hopi kinship patterns.

Hopi Clans

How do Hopi kinship patterns relate the Hopi to their world and hence to the sacred? The Hopi say that since their emergence they have been divided into a number of clans. Each clan traces its ancestry to some *wu'ya* (clan symbol, clan ancestor, or clan ancient), and as Mischa Titiev first noted, "the great majority of names on any clan list are those of plants, animals or supernatural personages."[9] A quick glance at any accurate listing of Hopi clans bears out Titiev's point.[10] There we find such names as bear, bluebird, spider, sun, eagle, greasewood, corn, tobacco, rabbit, coyote, yucca, badger, butterfly, snow, rain, cloud, sparrowhawk, crane, squash, duck, crow, parrot, spruce, reed, sand, lizard, and snake. Virtually all these phenomena are clearly visible in Hopiland, and the visible forms are considered descendants of the spiritual clan ancestors. The names of actual living clans vary a bit among the three mesas, but they are by and large quite consistent throughout Hopiland.[11]

To understand Hopi kinship patterns on the religious level one first needs to understand Hopi clan ancestors, a difficult task for the uninitiated. The Hopi speak with great affection and reverence about their clan ancestors and generally refer to them as "relatives" or "partners."[12] Fred Eggan was the first scholar to note that clan members feel they are related to the phenomena associated with their clan names. Sand clan members, for example, feel especially close to the earth, Corn clan members to corn, and Eagle clan members to eagles. The Hopi, unlike several other "totemic" peoples, do not generally feel that clan members are direct descendants of their ancients, but they nonetheless experience close ties with their clan ancestors. The clan system is the outstanding dimension of social life for the Hopi.[13] They define themselves primarily in terms of the revelations of their cosmos. Not only clan names but also Hopi proper names are taken from cosmic forms and linked in some way with the clans to which they belong. In addition, each Hopi belongs simultaneously to several clans by virtue of a principle of kinship that allows each Hopi to relate to several aspects of the world.

A good example is found in the social structural world of Don Talayesva, a Hopi whose autobiography, *Sun Chief*, has become a classic. He was born of the Sun clan. The name Talayesva was given to him by his ceremonial father after initiation into the Wuwtsim society, one of four Hopi men's ritual fraternities. Talayesva means "sitting tassel" and refers to the small tassels that sit on top of both bamboo and greasewood, clans to which Talayes-va's ceremonial father belonged. Indeed, Talayesva was linked socially to five different phratries (groups of clans that go together), each of which consisted of three or more clans. His clan affiliations through connecting relatives included sun, eagle, hawk, greasewood, bamboo, bow-arrow, roadrunner, sand, lizard, snake, fire, Maasaw, coyote, agave, cedar, badger, gray badger, butterfly, parrot, kachina, rabbit, and tobacco clans. Thus each Hopi is related through kinship ties to many varying aspects of the world.[14]

But the relationship is not simply natural. Unquestionably Hopi social structure "naturalizes" or "cosmicizes" humans, but it is essential to remember that spirit and matter are inseparably related for the Hopi and other Native Americans. Clan ancestors are natural, but they are also spiritual and eternal figures who first revealed themselves during the sacred history of Hopi clan migrations to the center. The religious character of the ancients is of such significance that Eggan asserted that the "conception of the clan as a 'timeless' and permanent group is fundamental to an understanding of Hopi social organization."[15] Being a Hopi clan member is in itself experienced religiously, for the Hopi, simply by being members of a clan, identify themselves fundamentally with their ancients. To be aware of one's relationship with various clan ancestors is to reexperience the sacred time when everything first came to be, an eternal era when all life and forms shared the same sacred essence. As Louis Hieb discovered, the Hopi do not say "I am of the same flesh and blood as my parents," but rather "I am the liquid substance of my father (ancestors)."[16]

Because the Hopi feel a great sense of relationship and even identity with their clan ancestors, their kinship patterns afford them the experience of transcendence over their strictly human status. To be a Hopi clan member is to relate to the world—and thus to the sacred, which is the source, sustenance, and end of the world. Some Hopis seem to relate more closely than others to the various aspects or dimensions of the sacred through the division into clans, but these divisions are ultimately transcended. The Hopi clans, through their divisive and material dimensions, paradoxically point beyond themselves to spheres of unity and spirituality. In the end, therefore, the Hopi clan system serves to relate and identify all Hopis with each other and their world.

At the same time, the religious experience of kinship has practical dimensions because the experience of one's clan membership recreates the world when the clans first came to be. Thus the Hopi, through their division into clans, paradoxically experience a sense of timeless unity with the world—which itself is practical, for the world is thereby renewed.

There is also a social practicality to Hopi clans, an "ordinary" religious dimension, to use Charles Long's term. Clans are part of the fabric of Hopi social structure, helping to organize daily and ritual activities. For the Hopi, the practicality of clans is assured because clans are religious in origin and nature. Clans work socially because they are sacred.

Hopi Phratries

An important Hopi phenomenon that interrelates kinship, agriculture, and religion is the phratry. Hopi phratries have received a great deal of attention from various scholars of Hopi life precisely because they embody a number of ranges of meaning. Furthermore, these multiple semantic levels are related to religiously meaningful everyday Hopi activities that secure material blessings. Hopi phratries thus prove to be quite illuminating in revealing the multidimensional meanings embodied by Hopis as they live their lives.[17]

Phratries are groups of clans linked together by a practical logic. The study of Hopi phratries is significant, for it reveals much about the way the Hopi classify their perceptions of the world. A number of studies have commented on Hopi classifications of nature, and most have emphasized the systematic and coherent character of Hopi categories.[18] This perspective has pictured the Hopi as supremely orderly and logical people who are almost devoid of the contradictions that mark human beings. Laura Thompson, for instance, described Hopi phratries as following an "ideal pattern" of associations.

Eggan was the first scholar to question the theory of a Hopi master plan of associations. In particular he criticized Thompson's proposed scheme on two grounds. First, he noted that the Hopi "never developed a central hierarchy of priests to organize and systematize the somewhat differing conceptions of the world which each clan or ceremonial group hold." Second, and more important, he argued that the Hopi classification of nature through the clan-phratry system is "based on the significant activities of Hopi life as related to the external environment." In other words, Hopi action embodies Hopi theory rather than following it. Eggan was keenly aware of the lack of systematic conceptualization in Hopi classificatory structures. He noted that the Hopi's thought world possesses a logic, but he said it is "Hopi logic," not Western logic. Realizing the link between Hopi logic and Hopi religion, Eggan called for "a much greater knowledge of Hopi ceremonies than we possess." While Titiev's *Old Oraibi* included a large section on Hopi ceremonialism, Eggan nonetheless asserted that no detailed interpretive account of any Hopi ritual existed in 1950.[19]

The Hopi, having no conceptual master plan of associations that interrelates all aspects of their life in a logically coherent manner, embody what Pierre Bordieu called "practical logic" and a "logic of the body," a logic that is lived. This logic, perhaps mythological, is concerned with living a long, healthy life and thus is quite practical. It operates in particular historical contexts, and so the axes of Hopi logic are apt to change from time to time. Life for the Hopi is to be lived, not conceptualized, though their actions do embody a cognitive operation. Bordieu captured this essential point, arguing that practical logic is

incomparably more ambiguous and more overdetermined than the most overdetermined uses of ordinary language. This is why ritual "roots" are always broader and vaguer than linguistic roots, and why the gymnastics of ritual, like dreams, always seem richer than the verbal translations that may be given of it. Words, however changed with connotation, limit the ranges of choices and render difficult or impossible . . . the relations which the language of the body suggests.[20]

Eggan was also the first scholar to note the practical significance of the grouping of Hopi clans into phratries. Each group of clans is linked by virtue of their relationship with similar natural phenomena that the Hopi hope to influence harmoniously through prayer. Each phratry is essentially tied to either farming or hunting and gathering. The Hopi phratries on Third Mesa concerned primarily with agricultural phenomena are Bear-Spider-Bluebird-Bear's Rope, Badger-Butterfly, Kachina-Parrot-Crow, Piikyas-Patki, Corn-Cloud-Rain, Snake-Sand-Lizard, and Sun-Eagle. The others, more concerned with hunting and gathering (though there is much overlap owing to the practical logic of the Hopi), are Reed-Greasewood-Bow-Arrow-Roadrunner, Fire-Coyote-Maasaw, Tobacco-Rabbit, and Squash-Sparrowhawk-Crane.

The Kachina-Parrot-Crow phratry receives mythological sanction from a number of oral traditions that relate kachinas, or spiritual beings, to parrots, crows, and spruce. According to one narrative, the Crow clan (which is related to crows) resided in the San Francisco Mountains, one of the present homes of the kachinas. The Crow clan discovered the kachinas there in the "long ago" and was given kachina rain dances in return for prayer sticks. Then the Crow clan became transformed into the Kachina clan while retaining the significance of the Crow clan through the Crow-Wing kachina. Eggan stated that "the Crow-Wing Katsina acts as 'mother' of the Katsinas during the Katsina initiation,"[21] and Bradfield said "she is wuya to the whole phratry."[22] In terms of perception, crows and ravens are associated with kachinas through their relationship with rain clouds, according to Eggan, "since they come in flocks an hour or two before a storm."[23]

Other mythical traditions hold that the kachinas originally came to Hopiland from the south and that Kachina clan members are descendants of the true kachinas.[24] Parrots are linked with kachinas, for Hopi tradition holds that they came with the kachinas from the south and offered their feathers to the kachinas to be used as headdress decorations. L. L. Hargrave even surmised that one species of parrot lived at one time in the pine forests of the San Francisco Mountains, though the evidence is scanty.[25] Still, the Parrot clan is clearly associated with kachinas, and the different colors represented by parrot feathers are prayers for rain. Each direction has its own color, and parrot feathers are prayer mediums that summon the rain from the direction associated with their color.

Other cosmic phenomena from which clan names in the phratry are derived are spruce and Douglas fir, both of which are found on the higher slopes of the San Francisco Mountains. Douglas fir is perceived to be a house of kachinas and a strong attractor of rain.[26] Also linked with water is the Cottonwood clan, named after the tree that grows near water whose wood is used to make Hopi prayer sticks.

Several birds have lent their names to associated clans, including the yellow warbler, the "sun maiden" (oriole), and the Utah red-winged blackbird. All are linked with the return of warm weather and the growing season.[27] For the Hopi, any yellow bird is linked with warm weather, rain, and fertility, for, as Stephen reported, "when there is no rain, there are no yellow birds; when there is plenty of rain, there are plenty of grass seeds and multitudes of yellow birds are seen eating the seeds and scattering the life-giving pollen over the land."[28] During Powamuya, warbler and oriole feathers are used ceremonially as prayers for the arrival of warm weather, and the Powamuy chief is said to symbolize the blackbird (tokotsqa).[29] The return of tokotsqa each spring signals the time to plant early corn, and thus the arrival of the Powamuy chief at the kivas signals the time to plant seeds in the heated kivas as a prayer for a successful upcoming harvest. In one winter ritual the Gray Flute society members stick four oriole feathers into a small ball of snow "so that the snow should melt and make the fields wet."[30]

Clearly the thread that links the clans of the Kachina-Parrot-Crow phratry is concern for rain, fertility, and warm weather. The kachinas return to the Hopi villages the day after the conclusion of Wuwtsim, and from then until they depart in late July they dance especially for rain and crop growth; indeed, Kennard stated that kachina songs are "really another medium in which the symbols for rain, corn fertility, and growth are expressed."[31] The Kachina-Parrot-Crow phratry, then, is related most closely to agricultural concerns and needs.

Different though interrelated associations are revealed by the Reed-Greasewood-Bow phratry. According to several narratives, the shrike and the mockingbird both played important roles during the Hopi's emergence to this world.[32] The shrike discovered the fourth world, and the mockingbird taught the Hopi their language as well as many sacred songs sung during Wuwtsim. Two clans are named for these birds, and another clan, Reed, takes its name from the plant used by humans to emerge from the underworld to this world.[33] Once the Hopi emerged, the Bow clan members brought the Wuwtsim ceremony to Third Mesa; that rite is concerned with reliving the emergence mythology and bringing rain.[34]

Bows are traditionally made from oak or shablow, from which come two more clan names in this phratry.[35] Arrows, while not actually represented by any clan, find expression at Oraibi in the Roadrunner clan, for the roadrunner is said to run fast "like an arrow."[36] The Reed clan is also linked with arrows because the reed was used by the Hopi and their Great Basin Shoshoni ancestors for arrow shafts.[37] The perceived association between the Reed clan and emergence is easily seen in many of the personal names received by Reed clan members; even more obvious are the associations between Reed and Bow clan names and arrows.[38]

Greasewood, from which another clan name comes, is used by the Hopi and the Great Basin Shoshoni for making planting sticks.[39] Planting sticks, besides recalling the humble life chosen in the beginning by the Hopi, are placed in the graves of deceased Hopis to serve as ladders to let the "breath body" emerge and travel to the land of the dead.[40] The link with the spiritual realm is important here, for the Wuwtsim ceremony is in part concerned with teaching initiates about the underworld.[41] The Star clan, found only on First Mesa,[42] takes its name from the stars in the sky, which, according to one myth, were made in the "long ago" by Coyote.[43] On Third Mesa, the War chief is chosen from the Coyote clan, which is significant because stars and coyotes are linked with war.[44]

The shrike, which found the place of emergence, is said to belong to the Warrior society. Shrikes are predators of grasshoppers, beetles, mice, and lizards, all of which live year round in the

Hopi region.[45] Shrikes sometimes appeared on Hopi war shields and were called "watchmen."[46] The mockingbird is not a predator like the shrike but is colored similarly.[47] It too played a significant part in the emergence of the Hopi by teaching them their language.[48] The Owl clan found in the Reed-Greasewood-Bow phratry takes its name from the great horned owl, another permanent resident of Hopi.[49] Like the shrike, the owl often appeared on Hopi war shields, where it was seen as a "scout with piercing eyes who finds the enemy at night."[50] Owl kachina symbolizes the conscience of the Hopi at clown ceremonies. Emory Sekaquaptewa stated that this kachina tries to persuade the clowns to change their "not Hopi" *(kahopi)* ways and follow his guide, but failing to do so, he calls in many Warrior kachinas, who whip the clowns severely and thereby "force the clowns to take responsibility for their actions."[51]

As Eggan noted, the clan names I have just reviewed are "intelligible in terms of the 'bow and arrow complex.' "[52] As such they are related to both hunting and warfare structures. Furthermore, they may well have had their origin in ancient Hopi hunting and gathering modes of being, for the Hopi share with the related Shoshoni hunters the basic word stems for bow and arrow.[53]

Only four clan names are related to Hopi material culture, and one of them is bow. The others are fire, carrying strap, and curved throwing stick. All four are related to fundamental activities of the hunting-gathering Great Basin Shoshoni and ancestral Hopi. All four relate to active decipherments of cosmic rhythms, though the activities related to them paradoxically point back to their passive, ultimate character. The gods upon which the Hopi depend gave all four implements directly or indirectly to the Hopi. Sun and Pöqangwhoya gave the bow and arrow, Maasaw gave the fire spindle, Kiisa gave the curved throwing stick, and Bear gave the carrying strap. Therefore none of these material cultural artifacts is perceived as the result of human initiative and creativity. True, each implement is used in a direct engagement with the world to do something—fire making, gathering, and hunting. However, the fruits acquired through the use of these tools are not understood as the creations of the Hopi because the Hopi feel they can receive only that which the world offers them. The fruits of the earth are created and offered by the gods, so the Hopi never emphasize their own activity in such contexts. In other words, Hopi activities point beyond themselves to structures of ultimacy and receptivity. The direct active confrontation of Hopis with their world through tasks such as hunting and fire making reveals the receptive character of their humanity.

Male and Female Sacred Activities

Even perception is an activity, though when viewed alongside subsistence modes it seems passive. In perception the Hopi decipher the revelations of a sacred environment, a cosmos that strikes them as ultimately powerful. Hopi activities are divided into lived modes, active and passive. Active forms are activities such as subsistence modes in which human exertion paradoxically reveals that humans are in the end passive and receptive. The material world resists human effort but eventually yields gifts. Passive modes of human activity such as perception operate a bit differently. There, human passivity, seeing but not confronting the world directly, reveals the ultimate power and activity of the world. When one looks upon the world one senses the power of life. In both cases, the Hopi experience passivity, in that the world makes them more than they make the world. It is this fundamental dimension of passivity or receptivity that Kennard referred to when he noted that the Hopi speak as though they do not act autonomously to control their own destinies: "Even when speaking English a Hopi does not say, 'I guess I'll have to change my way.' Instead he says, 'I guess I'll come to that.' "[54]

At a broad level which does not exclude overlap, it seems that these two modes of religious experience, active and passive, are embodied in differing degrees by men and women. In general, the passive experience of the world's autonomy is embodied more by women, or at least has a feminine character to it. Conversely, the active decipherment of the Hopi cosmos seems especially a male concern or embodies masculinity. The Hopi way of life emphasizes the passive experience of the world. Hopi social structure and mythology stress a rather passive, feminine experience of the world, and the basic Hopi perception of the sacred has a feminine, passive coloring. The active experience of the sacred, on the other hand, is essentially male in character as revealed in the four cultural implements from which clan names are taken. These implements relate to primordial hunting-gathering structures of meaning. The bow and arrow, the throwing stick, the fire spindle, and the carrying strap originated when the Hopi were predominantly hunter-gatherers. Furthermore, they all relate especially to male concerns and roles through which the sacred is experienced—to the hunt, which was and is a male's concern among the Hopi. To better understand this connection, the religious meaning of hunting for men needs explanation.

Women give birth to babies, and they do so through internal blood and internal space. This ability links women very closely to the earth mother, the primary locus of the sacred for the Hopi.[55] Hopi women are homologous to the earth mother because they too embody the most powerful and basic manifestation of the sacred, birth. The ability of Hopi women to be mothers is highly prized and confers on them a sense of worth that, in one sense, is more fundamental than that of men, although men are esteemed for their ceremonial commuication with the gods.[56] Hopi men do not participate directly in the birth process as women do, but they can participate in other creative processes symbolically through the hunt. In the hunt men shed blood external to themselves in external space in order to create new forms, that is, they give birth to meat, skins, furs, and other cultural artifacts (such as the carrying strap). One Hopi myth narrates that men and women were not living properly in the "long ago," so they were ordered to split up and live on different sides of a river. Both men and women grew corn, but only the men hunted, and eventually the women longed for meat and clothing.[57]

The Hopi association of hunting with external blood and external space is shown by a hunt ritual that traditionally took place on First and Second Mesas.[58] When a Hopi boy kills his first jackrabbit, the men choose the best hunter among them to act as "hunt father." All the hunters form a circle around the youth, who strips to the waist. The boy then bows to each of the four cardinal directions. Each time the youth bows, the hunt father draws the dead rabbit across his back, leaving a trail of blood. This ritual gesture symbolizes the hunt's link with external space and external blood. The meat and fur of the rabbit is born through the hunt. The boy then abstains from meat and salt for four days. On the morning of the fifth day, the boy receives a new name. The hunt father gives the lad two curved throwing sticks, then paints the boy with a broad yellow line across the chest from shoulder to shoulder, with short parallel lines above and below the elbows and knees. Two vertical lines of red ochre are painted on each cheek and the rest of the face is daubed with white cornmeal. The hunt father dresses similarly. The boy's new name is announced to the men, and a special hunt takes place.

The yellow stripes symbolize the markings of the sparrow hawk, to whom Hopi men are likened. The throwing stick is modeled after the sparrow hawk's wing and symbolizes Kiisa, the hawk who taught Hopi men how to hunt. The red ochre stripes on the boy's face symbolize the blood of the hunt, the blood that Hopi men shed in order to create life for the tribe. Thus through the hunt and its richly symbolic language, Hopi men experience that which the women experience in almost mute form simply by being women.

The Wuwtsim manhood initiation further teaches Hopi men the techniques and especially the religious meaning of hunting. The neophytes are likened to baby hawks, unable to fly from the nest until they learn the meaning of the hunt. At that point they become mature, and upon initiation into manhood they go on a rabbit hunt dressed in hawk outfits, giving the cry of the adult sparrow hawk.[59]

While Hopi men are likened to sparrow hawks (hunters), women are likened to butterflies, gentle creatures associated with the life-giving forces of the universe. Pubescent Hopi women prior to marriage traditionally wore their hair in butterfly whorls, symbolizing their creative potential,[60] and at marriage they are given a large and a small wedding robe as well as a complete wedding costume that embodies similar meanings. Edmund Nequatewa, a

Second Mesa Hopi, revealed that tassels are attached to each corner of the large Hopi wedding blanket, symbolic of female sacral powers of childbirth.[61] The tassel contains a small woven tube of black and white yarn, which represents the uterus. The feathers symbolize the souls or breath bodies of unborn children. A red yarn ring signifies the placenta, and red yarn the blood and veins in the uterus. The feminine character of these symbols is obvious and clearly differentiates female from male sacred activities in Hopi religious experience.

Still another major feature distinguishes Hopi male and female sacred activities. Mischa Titiev was the first to note that although the Hopi are divided into a number of named clans, they often err in assigning people to their proper clans. At the same time, the Hopi rarely err in assigning people to their proper phratries, which are composed of two or more clans.[62] The problem, Eggan noted, is further complicated by the fact that the phratry groupings are amazingly consistent, regardless of the clans actually present today. Eggan, and later R. Maitland Bradfield, demonstrated how Hopi phratries are virtually identical across all three mesas, a fascinating phenomenon given the differences in other aspects of life found between the mesas.[63] Eggan, however, provided the essential clue toward solving the clan-phratry problem when he noted that each phratry groups together aspects of nature that are important to Hopi life.[64] The practicality of the phratries relates especially to the ceremonial functions each phratry embodies. Each one (and again there is considerable overlap) is concerned with controlling, through prayer, the cosmic rhythms associated with its clans. The ceremonial concerns of the Hopi are quite consistent across all three mesas, which helps to explain why the phratries are so consistent despite the diversity of clans.

The phratry system and the related ceremonial calendar are primarily male concerns. Bradfield stated that the Hopi are more concerned with controlling events than with owning things and that, while Hopi clans are concerned with property rights, phratries are concerned with controlling certain desirable cosmic rhythms. His distinction between the concerns of Hopi clans and phratries seems valid, but the Hopi do not give precedence to the reality of events over the reality of things. Hopi ceremonies pertain more to controlling events than to owning things, but they are primarily the concern of men; Bradfield erred in generalizing this point to Hopi women.

Hopi clans are matrilineal. Hopi women own farm lands, houses, cisterns, and even the sacred *tiiponi*, the "heart" of each major male ritual, all of which are passed along according to kinship. As some Hopi men once wrote, "the family, the dwelling house and field are inseparable, because the woman is the heart of these, they rest with her."[66] Hopi women embody sacredness almost mutely through the concrete, internal phenomena of birth, kinship structures, the property rights; Hopi men express sacredness through the symbolic, external language of hunting and ceremonies, especially as they relate to Hopi emergence mythology.

Hopi Rites of Passage

It is reasonable to say that, on one plane, the Hopi understand their origin, nature, and destiny in terms of plant life, especially corn. Indeed, Hopi and non-Hopi scholars alike have said so. Furthermore, corn is linked especially with female religiosity— which should hardly be surprising, given the female character of the Hopi emergence mythology that farming recalls. As Mary Black demonstrated, however, corn is a symbol for all Hopis, male and female.[67] Like the corn on which they subsist, the Hopi were born of the earth. Even initiated males are likened to mature or ripe corn (as well as to full-grown hawks ready to fly from the nest).

The homologies, or structural parallels, between corn and the Hopi begin with the birth of a child and relate birth to agriculture and mythology. When a Hopi child is born, he or she is kept inside the house for twenty days, away from the sun's light.[68] Walter C. O'Kane recorded the remarks made by a Hopi who explained this ritual:

> If you plant a seed in the ground . . . it will be about ten days before the little plant first shows above the surface. Sometimes a little less, sometimes a little more. But about ten days.

The plant as it first appears, though, is not just like it will be a little later. It does not yet have the right leaves. Its shape is not quite right. It has made a start, and if it can live and grow a little more and not suffer any harm, it will be the way it ought to be. But it must be protected. The hot sun must not shine on it while it is so little and tender. Otherwise it may die.

Another ten days are necessary, so that it may gain strength. At the end of that time it will still be only a little plant, but it will be like it is going to be as it grows larger. It will have the kind of leaves that are right for it. It will not be harmed if the sun shines on it.

A baby is like a plant that has started to grow from a seed. It must be protected in just the same way. It needs the ten days that were required while the seed was sending the little plant up to the surface of the ground, and the other ten days while the right leaves were forming. For twenty days the sun must not shine on it. Then on the twenty-first day its mother takes it in her arms, and along with her mother, or some other woman, carries it out of the house to the edge of the mesa and there prays for its health and happiness. On that day the baby is given its name.

This . . . is the reason why the windows of a house are covered where a baby has just been born.[69]

The connections between corn seeds and sprouts on one hand and newborns on the other are evident. Yet at the same time the twenty-day confinement period is understood as a reenactment of the emergence myth, the darkened room symbolizing the underworld from which the Hopi emerged in the beginning.[70] The baby when born is perceived by the Hopi to be incomplete, just as the first Hopis were in the underworld. According to tradition, Hopis in the underworld underwent a metamorphosis from insectlike creatures to fully human beings who finally emerged to this world. The stages of transformation undergone by the Hopi are symbolized by four worlds, three being underground, the fourth being this world. The twenty-day confinement period following a birth is divided into four periods of five days each, symbolic of previous worlds. The day after birth, the attendant rubs four lines of "sacred cornmeal" (*homngumni*, or *hooma*) onto the four walls of the room, each one about an inch wide and six inches long.[71] Then at sunrise on the tenth, fifteenth, and twentieth days, one cornmeal line is removed to symbolize the transition of the infant from one world to another. At sunrise on the twentieth day, the baby is considered to have emerged to this world and is taken outside to the mesa edge to be presented for the first time to the sun. Hopi oral tradition holds that there was no light in the underworld and that the Hopi helped ritually create the sun only after they had emerged to the fourth world.[72] The presentation of a twenty-day-old infant to the sun is likened to the emergence of the Hopi through the earth navel. Hence birth is likened to the planting and germination of seeds and simultaneously symbolizes the formation of the Hopi world.

During the Wuwtsim ceremony, Hopi males are also homologized with corn plants in a way that recalls their emergence.[73] The Wuwtsim initiation into one of four religious societies reenacts the Hopi cosmogony over a four-day period. According to Nequatewa, Wuwtsim "portrays what happened in the Underworld before the Hopi people emerged and what they did to get out."[74] The Wuwtsim ceremony is secret and parts have never been viewed by outsiders, but several Hopis have confirmed Nequatewa's interpretation.[75] The initiation of Hopi youth into adulthood involves the experience of their origin as people. In other words, to be a Hopi is to reexperience the sacred history of their cosmogony and to learn of the sacred dimension of their world. The Hopi who complete their initiation into adulthood by understanding that a spiritual dimension pervades their world are said to be "ripe" or "mature" (hoyya), another homology between the Hopi and the corn which is their subsistence.[76] Planting corn is also likened to teaching sacred traditions, another part of Wuwtsim. Milland Lomakema, a Second Mesa Hopi, demonstrated this connection in a statement in which he related corn, farming, sacred traditions, and ritual life: "In Hopi belief, if you want to teach a person the history or the song that is deeply connected to our history, you feed them corn. You're planting history into his person. Planting is really a life of Hopi."[77]

It should be noted that the Hopi do not think they are literally the world that they experience. The homologies drawn by the Hopi between themselves and their world are symbolic. This view is supported by a conversation between a ceremonial father and his son following the son's initiation into Wuwtsim. The conversation, which according to Edward Kennard, who recorded it, is very typical, indicates the pervasive character of symbolic understanding among adult Hopi:

"You really have become corn." . . . "If you have that as flesh, why do I have that as flesh?" "It is not that you have become real corn. . . . You have been nursing [sucking] on our mother [earth] for everything here grows up from below. . . . Whenever one plants seeds, they sprout. . . . After a while it appears above the ground. . . . Then it rains on it, and with its juice [moisture] makes it grow. . . . When it has eyes [kernels] it becomes ripe. . . . One makes his flesh with that. . . . When one goes back home [to earth, by dying] this body is a stalk. . . . By itself it is no longer useful. . . . And afterwards, the breath forms life. . . . That is what always lives. . . . That is what you are preparing for in your life. . . ."[78]

The Hopi are likened to corn both materially and spiritually. Materially, the Hopi perceive their bodies to be like stalks of corn, ephemeral and transitory. Indeed, the Hopi word *qatungwu*[79] refers both to a human corpse and a harvested corn plant. That which endures is the spiritual substance (breath, moisture) that constitutes all life and all forms and hence unifies all of creation. It is clear that the Hopi do not think they are "real corn" but rather that they are structurally like corn, both materially and spiritually. Hence they are aware of their own humanity even as they transcend it through their experience of relationship with the world.

Practical activities, kinship classifications, and perception all evoke the experience of sacredness among the Hopi. Paradoxically, to be a Hopi is to experience transcendence over time and space by and through the Hopi's orientation within time and space. The Hopi were created in the timeless time of the emergence and thus to be Hopi is to reexperience the primordium when all was created anew. By embodying specifically human characteristics created in the "long ago," the Hopi experience their unity with the sacred, for at that time, as Alexander Stephen noted, "the whole universe was endowed with the same breath (spiritual substance)—rocks, trees, grass, earth, all animals and men."[80] Because all was of one spiritual substance in the long ago the Hopi say that "when they came out all could speak to each, the animals and all vegetation."[81] All life and forms were harmoniously related to each other and to the source of life itself; it was a time when everything in the world shared a fertile and healthy life. On the ordinary, cultural level, rites of passage assure young Hopis of maturation, a practical development—but again one that is understood in religious terms. Hopi activities such as perception, subsistence pursuits, social behavior, and rites of passage have practical value precisely because they are experienced religiously.

Three

The Utility of Prayer

In the first draft of this chapter I used the Hopi Soyalangw ritual to demonstrate the religious character of the practical fruits of Hopi ceremonialism. Soyalangw, according to the Hopi, is "one of the most sacred ceremonies,"[1] because "everything branches out from the Soyal."[2] It is essentially the completion of the celebration of the Hopi new year, which begins in November with Wuwtsim. During Soyalangw the sun is turned back toward its summer home, and the complete sequence of significant events for the coming year is laid out symbolically. When I discussed the draft with a Hopi consultant on Third Mesa, however, he suggested that I might instead look at the Powamuya ritual, given its vital role in Hopi religion today.

At first I was a bit confused; why shouldn't I discuss Soyalangw? As I thought further about the matter I realized that Soyalangw is performed in its traditional form only on Second Mesa. It is no longer performed at all on First Mesa and is conducted only in abbreviated form on Third Mesa. Since the breakup of Old Oraibi village in 1906 and the subsequent formation of three new villages—Kikotsmovi, Hotevilla, and Bacavi—the Third Mesa priesthood has been split up, and no one village there can perform Soyalangw in its long form. Hence my discussion of Soyalangw was based on data that no longer describe the situation on Third Mesa, my primary area of focus.

Powamuya apparently remains basically unchanged on Third Mesa, however, and the data gathered by ethnologists at the turn of the century remains more or less accurate. In addition, the Kachina cult that is involved in this ritual is now more important than ever among the Hopi. And whereas the Wuwtsim initiations into adulthood were once considered essential for Hopi men, the Kachina and Powamuy initiations during Powamuya now seem to be all that is necessary, at least on First and Third Mesas. Thus Powamuya has become the most significant winter ceremony for the Hopi, performed on all three mesas.

Peter Whiteley was told by a clan elder from Hotevilla, the Third Mesa village that has preserved more rites than any other, that the ceremonies performed at Hotevilla embodied only a cultural dimension, with no real religious power.[3] This comment raises the question of whether my interpretation of the importance of Powamuya is appropriate for Third Mesa Hopis after 1906. The Hopi consultant who recommended that I discuss Powamuya is a clan relative to the elder cited by Whiteley, however, and is thoroughly familiar with Third Mesa prophecy. His implication, or at least my perception of it, is that Powamuya is still conducted in traditional form and is still perceived as a sacred rite. In addition, I have heard him say that one of his nephews dances kachina "with the proper attitude," again implying that kachina dances still embody a spiritual dimension. I have heard another Third Mesa prophecy holding that the kachina dances would be the last formal rites to die out,[4] and it is instructive to note that even the villages of Oraibi and Bacavi, after several years of nonperformance, have revived kachina dances in the past few years. I have also heard from Hopis that the only difference between the ceremonial calendar at Shongopavi, where most rites are still performed in traditional long form, and the calendar at Hotevilla is that Shongopavi does the rites "in a big way," implying a difference of form only. It may well be that Hopi religion is not reducible to a particular form. All ceremonies stress above all else the importance of participation with a "good heart" (lolma' unangwa), the form of the rite being the medium through which spritual powers are employed.

That religion is alive on Third Mesa is further supported by Whiteley's field notes, in which a Third Mesa elder recounts a prophecy holding that prayer through smoking and cornmeal sprinkling would remain with the Hopi after the formal ritual cycle was terminated.[5] The authenticity of religious rites on Third Mesa is also supported by the same Hotevilla clan elder who told Whiteley that ceremonies there retained only a cultural element: in another context he warned of very severe consequences resulting from the performance of Hopi rites while intoxicated, stating that impure thoughts could bring disease upon a person through the retribution of the sacred power of the ceremonies. Finally, the fact that Hopis on Third Mesa do not publicly talk about rites such as Powamuya shows that the rites are very much alive and well. In fact, it is for that reason that I limit my discussion of these rites to previously published accounts.

Besides, religion and culture are so indissolubly linked in the Hopi way that it is difficult to imagine ceremonies being performed at a cultural level only. It is even questionable whether separation of religion and culture is possible among Hopis, except within a larger and more fundamental context of relationship. It seems to me that Third Mesa Hopis view ceremonialism as existent or non-existent in relation to the context in which it is perceived. Insofar as they recognize twentieth-century cultural change as unique and unprecedented, they feel that their ritual calendar has been extinguished at a basic religious level. At the level of mythic continuity, however, Third Mesa Hopis feel that the sacred essence of the ceremonies remains unchanged and always will. Such a paradoxical interpretation may help us to understand the contrary behavior of Tawaquaptewa, who was the village chief (kikmongwi) of Oraibi during the time of the village split. Tawaquaptewa no doubt thought the split ended ceremonialism, as evidenced by his sullen disposition in later years and by his being buried as Ewtoto, chief of all kachinas. Yet in 1909, after he returned to Hopi from a three-year stay at Riverside, California, he held the Wuwtsim initiation (natnga), the major traditional tribal initiation rite for men.

The ambivalence toward the authenticity of religion among Third Mesa Hopis surrounds only the formal ceremonies (wiiwimi). Almost all prophecies hold that ritual smoking and cornmeal sprinkling will survive forever, indicating that religious experience and expression will always exist among Hopis. I say "almost all prophecies" because some Hopis interpret *wiiwimi* as pertaining to all practices of the Hopi way rather than just the ceremonial calendar in the strict sense. Furthermore, some of these same Hopis emphasize the prophecy that foretells the end of *wiiwimi* on Third Mesa, so that by extension they feel that all Hopi practices should be stopped.[6] But I believe that these Hopis are a small minority, and thus it is fair to say at a general level that Third Mesa Hopis still affirm the religious validity of basic prayer rites.

Hopi Prayer

In Hopi eyes, it is primarily prayer that brings to fruition a successful agricultural harvest. That such an understanding still persists among the Hopi is borne out by my many Hopi consultants as well as by the former tribal chairman Abbot Sekaquaptewa, who wrote a few years ago that

> fall in Hopi country nearly always brings with it the joy and celebration of a bountiful harvest, fulfilling for many industrious Hopis their prayers and aspirations set in the winter ceremonial rehearsals.
> . . .
> It has not been too long since famine was a part of the Hopi way; not because the common people made it so, but because mortal man in all his shortcomings did not always have a faith strong enough nor behavior humble enough to merit the blessing of lifegiving rain on this semi-arid land.[7]

These remarks clearly reveal the way in which the Hopi perceive prayer to be the essential work that brings about a successful harvest. As stated several times by the Hopi themselves, the entire ceremonial calendar is concerned with practical, material blessings, such as precipitation, long life, fertility, and good health. Just as practice is religious, religion is practical for the Hopi and other Native Americans. Religion is not simply imaginative; it is life giving and life sustaining, qualities that are simultaneously perceived religiously, for the sacred created the cosmos. As an initiated Third Mesa Hopi once told me, the making of all Hopi prayer offerings is referred to as *tumala* (work) or *tumala'ta* (work done). The Hopi perceive ritual prayer as work, that is, as an activity whose goal is the creation and sustenance of life in this world. Indeed, as Don Talayesva of Old Oraibi once said, prayer stick *(paaho)* construction is "the most important work in the world."[8] If it is not done properly, another writer noted, "life for the Hopi might end."[9]

Hopi prayer acts always involve material and spiritual dimensions, both of which must be harmoniously related if a prayer is to bear fruit.[10] Emory Sekaquaptewa explained to me the meaning of two terms often used to describe the spiritual and material dimensions of Hopi prayer. He stated that *naawakna* means to wish and will for a desired event and that *natwanta* means to act out symbolically the desired event. *Naawakna* refers to the spiritual aspect of Hopi prayer, while *natwanta* refers to the material aspects of Hopi prayer. The Hopi generally breathe their prayers onto some material object that symbolizes what they desire, primarily life-yielding moisture. It is well known that Hopis and other Native Americans perform a number of rituals for the primary purpose of acquiring rainfall. For the Hopi, rain—or rather the "spiritual substance" of rain—is perceived to be the constitutive, underlying structure of all the world's forms and rhythms. When the Hopi dance for rain, they are dancing (praying) for the creation and sustenance of the cosmos.

Sam Gill seemed to be very much aware of the practical importance of Hopi rituals when he noted that they are "nothing short of giving life."[11] At the same time, questions of interpretation are raised when Gill adds that rain is necessary for the maintenance of life in the desert regions of the southwestern United States. Rain is, of course, essential for Hopi survival, but not simply because the Hopi live in a semiarid region. The significance of rain for the Hopi is inseparably related to their experience of the sacred, so that rain would be sacred even if the Hopi climate was as wet as a rain forest. It is the "spiritual substance" within rain—not rain itself—that gives life to the Hopi world. Rain manifests the "very something," the creative power that yields life and being.

Preparing for Powamuya

Powamuya, sometimes called the Bean Dance, is the first major winter ritual following Soyalangw. Like Wuwtsim and Soyalangw, Powamuya has both long and short forms, the long forms occurring when initiations into the Kachina and Powamuy societies are to be held. When the Powamuy chief, traditionally a Badger clan member, first spots the February moon (Powamuya), he calls together the special officers for a preliminary prayer rite called Powalawu.[12] Occurring eight days before the main rite, Powalawu has as its purpose the preparation of the many prayer offerings to be used during Powamuya.

Ritual Smoking

To begin, the priests go to a kiva (an underground ceremonial chamber) to smoke ritually for rain.[13] Ritual smoking is perhaps the most common mode of prayer for Hopi men. It involves the smoking of Hopi wild tobacco mixed with rain tobacco (*yoyviva*) or spruce, pine, and aspen in a variety of clay pipes with reed stems. The participants sit in a semicircle, and each one "drinks" four puffs of smoke from the pipe, which is then passed to the next person. As the pipe changes hands, the two men involved exchange kinship terms—for example, "my father–my son," "my uncle–my nephew"—thus demonstrating the unity of their hearts in requesting material blessings from the sacred.

The Hopi feel that prayers are effective only if the participants are united in their thoughts and feelings, which should be focused on harmony and fertility for all the world. They also think that one participant with bad feelings, such as anger, greed, or arrogance, can ruin the efficacy of Hopi prayer. All Hopi prayer acts paradoxically embody the supplication of and participation in the sacred source of life. Prayer sticks (*paavaho*), breath feathers (*nakwakwusi*), sacred cornmeal (*homngumni*, or *hooma*), and ritual smoke are all perceived on one level as offerings to the gods. The gods are said to inhale the odor or essence (spiritual dimension) of the material offering, which, if offered with a good heart, is reciprocated with the blessing of rain, fertility, and health. At another level, the material medium through which the Hopi direct their prayers is understood as a microcosm of that which they desire. The Hopi feel that they embody a spark of the sacred, symbolized by breath (*hikwsi*), and can, at proper times, align that embodied essence with the sacred itself in order to participate in the rhythms of their cosmos. Thus the Hopi pray in two separate but interrelated ways: supplication and participation.

On the supplicatory level, which presupposes the transcendence or distance of the sacred from the Hopi, they offer the gods a gift of tobacco with the wish that the gods will repay them with rain. Conversely, at the participatory level, which assumes the immanence or relation of the sacred to themselves, or more specifically to their breath bodies, the Hopi attempt to participate in the rhythms of the sacred by focusing their spiritual essences on some material, microcosmic medium symbolic of that which they desire. Because Hopi prayer requires a proper union of spiritual and material dimensions, *naawakna* and *natwanta*, the Hopi must focus their hearts and minds on something physical and material. Hopi prayer acts are consistent with the Hopi's basic religious perception of the world, that the spiritual manifests itself through the material and the material manifests itself by virtue of its relationship with the spiritual.

Prayer Sticks and Breath Feathers

After smoking together, the Powamuy and Kachina chiefs retire to the northwest corner of the kiva to make prayer sticks and breath feathers. Prayer sticks are wooden sticks of varying lengths that are adorned with various herbs and feathers and a small corn husk packet containing grass seed, a pinch of cornmeal, a pinch of pollen, and a drop of honey.

The feathers, grasses, and plants vary depending on the particular blessing, in addition to moisture, that is sought. During Powalawu, sprigs of snakeweed and mountain sagebrush are attached. Powamuya is in part a prayer for warm weather, and warm weather is needed to grow snakeweed and mountain sagebrush. Also attached to the prayer sticks are single feathers of the blackbird, whose arrival in spring heralds the coming of warm weather. The corn husk packet represents a prayer that the earth, "Our Mother," will bring forth plenty of moisture and warmth in order to secure a bountiful harvest for the Hopi. Finally, yet most important, each prayer stick contains a breath feather, a downy eagle breast feather attached to a piece of string, symbolizing the breath of life and falling rain.[14]

The lightness of the downy feathers symbolizes the spiritual plane, immanent in all creation. The spiritual realm is an aspect of moisture, and thus the breath feather is above all a prayer that moisture, especially rain, will appear so that the world may be renewed. Prayer sticks are simultaneously offerings and spiritual instruments. The gods decorate their foreheads with them, and the Hopi concentrate their prayers through them.

The Sand Mosaic and Tiiponi

While the Powamuy and Kachina chiefs smoke and construct prayer sticks and breath feathers, the other priests construct a sand mosaic for a rite to consecrate the prayer offerings. The most prominent aspect of the sand painting is the solar symbol in the center, again revealing Powamuya's concern for warmth.[15]

Around the sand mosaic are placed various ritual objects. Clay stands are placed at each of the four cardinal directions and into them are inserted "small wooden crooks" (ngölöshooya) with turkey feathers attached to symbolize "life in its various stages" and as a prayer that all Hopis will grow to be old and bent over.[16] Also inserted into the clay stands are prayer sticks "representing corn, the main subsistence of the Hopi," in hopes of a successful harvest. Sprigs of the four kinds of shrubs used by the Hopi as windbreaks are also placed in the stands as a "prayer or wish for protection of the plants against the destructive sand storms." Next to each sprig are placed an eagle feather and four flycatcher feathers, "as a prayer for warm weather when the birds come."

The War chief is symbolized on a prayer stick called taqavaho (man prayer stick), the purpose of which is to keep watch over and protect the altar.[17] The Powamuya altar also contains four single reeds painted yellow; these reeds contain corn pollen, some oriole feathers, and some corn dough balls, which serve as food for the Six-Point-Cloud-People, who send rain.

Behind the sand mosaic stands the Powamuy chief's *tiiponi*. The *tiiponi* is the most sacred of all Hopi ritual objects. Each Hopi clan "owns" a *tiiponi*, which is kept by the head clan woman until needed for ritual use. But the meaning of the *tiiponi* outruns its particular clan, for the *tiiponi* is symbolic of the earth mother, the mother or grandmother of all Hopis.[18] Moreover, the *tiiponi* is symbolic of the cosmic totality, typically referred to by Hopis as the earth mother and sun father, for the feathers included in the *tiiponi* are symbolic of the sun's pets, the birds of the sky.[19] When discussing the *tiiponi* the Hopi generally refer only to its female sacred aspect, though the male dimension is implied. Because the Hopi cosmogony centers on creation from the womb of the earth, it is fair to say that the Hopi in some sense perceive the female sacred dimension to be the most fundamental, perhaps a very archaic understanding.

Alexander Stephen gave a good description of the Hopi understanding of the *tiiponi*:

> The tiiponi were first obtained in the Underworld. . . . It is the mother of the people; in the interior are the seeds of all edible vegetation, all garden products, pinon nuts, cedar berries, every kind known to the Hopi. The feathers are eagle, turkey, parroquet, yellow bird, all birds are typified or embraced. The cotton string wrapping is the garment; the bits of mother of pearl, turquoise, etc., tied around it to typify wealth. The ridge is the Hopi land in which they are set. The puhtabi (road prayer feather) is the trail over which travel all the prayers of all the people, old men and young, women and children. . . . When the people traveled in the early migrations, it guarded them.[20]

Near the *tiiponi* are placed four black reeds containing some specular iron and a few bluebird feathers. There is a bone whistle to summon the Cloud People from each of the six directions. Four clay balls with flint spearheads symbolize Pöqangwhoya, the elder Hopi war god, who instills in Hopis bravery, strength, and good health.[21] There are also a corn husk with a dead mouse attached, breath feathers, sacred cornmeal, and medicine water (*nqaakuyi*).

Medicine Water and Hopi Logic

To make medicine water, a ray of sunlight, symbolizing the sacredness of "above" and "male," is refracted through quartz into a bowl of spring water, which symbolizes "below" and "female." This act unites heaven and earth, male and female, and is a powerful prayer for creation and fertility. By making medicine water, the Hopi fructify the earth. Hopi mythology describes the primordial union of male and female gods from which life emerged. Different versions mention different gods. But the Hopi perceived no problem in stating that creation is the result of the union of a number of different deities, given that all deities are for them so many refractions of the "spiritual substance."

The Hopi say that in the beginning, in the "long ago," *Sootukwnangw* (Star God) married *Tuwapongtumsi* (Sand-Altar-Maiden), and "when they have intercourse, we get rain, for that is the fertilizing fluid."[22] Taawa (Sun) is also linked to fertilization. The warm rays of the sun are perceived by the Hopi as fertilizing the soil of the earth mother.[23] The earth mother, Tuwapongtumsi, is also linked with water and Water Serpent, Paalölögangw, who is male/female and who sends forth water from the below to form clouds.[24] Muy'ingwa, or Cloud, the god of germination, is generally considered male, but he is the chief of all clouds, there being a cloud associated with each direction. Star God is also closely associated with Sun, for he manifests himself as lightning, which is said to make the ground warm and hence fertile when it strikes.[25] Star God is closely related to Water Serpent, as evidenced by prayers offered to Water Serpent to ask Cloud to send fertile lightning.[26] Indeed, Stephen reproduced a Hopi rock engraving that shows several lightning bolts (symbolized by zigzag snake patterns) nursing from the breasts of a cloud in the form of Water Serpent.[27]

While these associations are no doubt loosely held together in terms of conceptual logic, Hopi logic is a lived logic that handles them rather easily. Hopi logic operates on the level of living religiously, and its axes are adjusted to its particular needs at specific times. In general the Hopi perceive the sky as male and the earth as female. If the Hopi direct their attention to the sky, however, it becomes both male (Sun, Star God) and female (Water Serpent). Similarly, while the earth is understood to be female in relation to the sky, a closer examination reveals that the earth has both female (Sand-Altar-Maiden) and male (germination god) aspects. In fact, the Hopi seem to make a mockery of all attempts to limit their logic through fixed, unchangeable axes. Hopi corn, for example, is often linked with the earth in an inseparable way, so that the Hopi refer to both as "Our Mother."[28] I have also read a Hopi myth, however, in which each separate type of corn was perceived to be an unmarried male.[29] And what is to be made of the fact that Hopi men do the hunting and yet the master of animals is perceived to be female (Tiikuywuuti, Child Sliding Out Woman)?[30]

Hopi logic is most concerned with living a long, healthy, meaningful life, not with some intellectual and analytical conceptualization of the world. For the Hopi, meaning is situated within practical contexts that do not exclude contradiction. In making medicine water, for instance, the sky is associated with the sun and is linked with warmth in contrast to the below, which is associated with water and coldness. When the Hopi associate the sky with the hawk, the hunt, and maleness, however, the sky is linked with the coldness of winter, the time when Hopi men generally hunt. In fact, Bradfield argued that the winter ceremonies Wuwtsim, Soyalangw, and Momtcit stress male concerns of hunting and warfare while Powamuya, Home Dance, and the summer rites of Snake-Antelope, Flute, Maraw, Lakon, and Owaqöl stress female activities related to childbirth and agriculture.[31] In that sense Star God is linked to the above and winter, whereas in his association with the sun as lightning he is linked to the above and warmth. Furthermore, hunting and warfare are not necessarily related to coldness, for numerous Hopi myths relate that the eldest child of the sun is Pöqangwhoya, the elder war god, who taught the Hopi warfare and hunting.[32]

Prayer Songs

After the making of medicine water, all kiva members sit around the altar. The Tobacco chief lights a pipe filled with rain tobacco and passes it first to the Powamuy chief. All smoke silently and reverently. Then the Powamuy chief utters a brief prayer, and twelve prayer songs are sung in succession.

The first six songs are addressed to the Six-Point-Cloud-People as requests for rain. The seventh is devoted to many types of seeds and involves the Powamuy chief, who breathes a prayer for good crops onto sacred cornmeal and sprinkles it over the altar. During the eighth song, which is concerned with various medicinal herbs and wild vegetables, the Powamuy chief sprinkles the sand mosaic with medicine water. The chief symbolizes Muy'ingwa in this ritual act, for Muy'ingwa, as Cloud, is said to dip his great sprinkler, made of the feathers of birds, into the heavenly lakes to bring forth sweet rains.[33]

As the ninth song begins, the Powamuy chief's deputy takes the yellow reed tube from the northwest side of the altar as well as the bone whistle and climbs the kiva ladder halfway. He blows the corn pollen and oriole feathers to the northwest, following with a few notes on the whistle. He repeats the process with the other yellow tubes in the other cardinal directions and then does the same with the black reed tubes during the tenth song. The yellow and blue feathers embody a prayer for warm weather, when the summer birds arrive.[34] Prayers are offered to each of the four directions so that the Cloud People might visit the Hopi with the blessing of moisture from all directions.

Next the Powamuy chief takes the flint spearhead at the northwest direction and puts honey on it. He climbs the ladder halfway, licks off the honey, and spits (offers) it to each of the four directions. During the eleventh song, a messenger departs with the four clay balls and four breath feathers for a trail leading to the southwest. He carries offerings to *Huukyangw*, the dreaded god who appears in high winds and sand storms.[35] The prayer offerings are deposited to the southwest of the village because the sand storms generally arrive from the southwest and either cover the crops or cut them down.

While the twelfth song proceeds, each of four messengers takes a clay stand, dough ball, and reed tube from one of the four directions and leaves the kiva, heading out of the village, each in a different cardinal direction. Then the four hold some meal to their mouths, breathe on it a prayer for moisture and creation, and sprinkle the meal in a line toward the village. They place the clay stand at the end, pointing toward the village. The dough ball and reed are aligned toward the proper cardinal direction, and the messengers proceed back to the kiva. Their actions both petition and summon the Cloud People to come from each direction to visit the village with moisture. Meanwhile another messenger takes the corn husk containing sacred meal and a dead mouse to a large anthill as an offering to the ants so that they will not destroy the crops.[36] Upon returning, all smoke again.

Planting Beans and Corn

At sunrise the next morning, the Powamuy chief, symbolizing *tokotsqa* (blackbird), visits each kiva and, facing east, smokes with the kiva head. The chief then gives the kiva head a prayer stick with blackbird feathers and tells him that he may now begin planting beans. Just as the arrival of the blackbird each spring signifies the time to plant corn, so the chief's arrival signifies the time to plant beans in the kiva in order to "ritually plan" (*pasiuni*) the coming crop harvest.[37] From then until the end of Powamuya a fire is kept bazing to grow fifty to one hundred bean sprouts in each kiva.

The beans are grown for the kachinas Ewtoto and Ahooli.[38] Ewtoto, the chief kachina, is ancestral to the Bear clan, while Ahooli, seen only on Third Mesa, is a *wu'ya* (ancient, ancestor) to the Piikyas, or Young Corn clan.[39] Ewtoto is the spiritual counterpart to the village chief (on Second and Third Mesas), who impersonates him. The Piikyas chief, who is assistant chief during Soyalangw, impersonates Ahooli, who is second in importance to Ewtoto. While the other Powamuy members plant beans, the

Powamuy chief, Ewtoto (the village chief), and Ahooli (the Piikyas chief) plant corn.

From planting time until harvest, Patsavu Hu' kachinas patrol the kivas to inspect the sprouts and thrash with yucca blades anyone who is caught lying down or sleeping. The Hopi perceive Powamuya as a continuous prayer, and so all are required to be awake and alert, with strong and good thoughts about crop germination and growth. To be drowsy or asleep slows crop growth; lazy attendants are awakened by the sting of yucca blades. Yucca is also understood by the Hopi to be a purifying substance, and anyone who is whipped by the kachinas is understood to be purified of misdeeds. Most participants are eager to grow a successful kiva crop because it not only reveals good hearts but also forecasts a fruitful fall harvest.[40]

The bean and corn shoots are understood as prayer offerings on one level, but on another level they are the microcosmic medium through which the Hopi can focus their breath bodies in order to will a bountiful autumn harvest. To facilitate the growth of the sprouts, informal kachina dances and rehearsals of the Bean Dance are held during the interval between Powalawu and Powamuya. The shoots are watered periodically as a prayer that rain might feed the crops in the upcoming season.

Powamuya

At sunrise eight days after Powalawu, Powamuya begins as the Powamuy chief and the Kachina chief set up the na'tsi (standard) outside the kiva hatch. Little happens on the first four days of the rite. The standard is set up each morning, and two leaders smoke silently several times during the day. On the second day, the Powamuy chief visits all the other kivas to smoke and bless the bean sprouts and to announce that the Powamuy kachinas will arrive and dance on the eighth night.

The Initiations

Every three or four years, the fifth and sixth days of Powamuya are devoted primarily to the Powamuy and the Kachina societies' initiations. By tradition, all Hopi children who have turned seven or eight years old in the preceding year are initiated into one of these religious societies.[41]

THE POWAMUY SOCIETY

The initiation observances for the Powamuy society begin on the fifth day of Powamuya. An altar is constructed containing medicine water; a chief's jug; *tiiponi;* sacred cornmeal; corn, cloud, and rain symbols; two Hu' kachinas; Poqangwhoya (elder war god); and Tcowilawu, ancestor to the Badger clan. The chief's jug *(mong-wikoro),* made of netted clay and about five inches high and fourteen inches in circumference, is a powerful prayer for rain.[42] It is used to gather sacred water from various kachina shrines (springs); the priests also use it to pray for rain by pouring water onto some object that represents an aspect of Hopiland. The pouring of water from the chief's jug by a priest is a ritual event that forecasts rain on the cosmic level. Tcowilawu, who seems to be seen only on Third Mesa, is closely related or identical to Muy'ingwa (Cloud). The sand mosaic features numerous cloud and squash blossom designs, and a small Powamuy altar is also present. It contains a *tiiponi,* some sacred cornmeal, three sticks with breath feathers attached, and a medicine water bowl, around which are placed six colored ears of corn. These ears are symbolic, "chromatic" prayers, twice over.[43] They represent the major types (colors) of corn and beans grown by the Hopi and the colors of the Six-Point-Cloud-People. Hence these ears are a prayer that rain will come from all directions to make the upcoming harvest plentiful.

When the novices enter the kiva with their ceremonial parents, each one throws a little cornmeal toward the altar and is then seated at the raised (profane) end of the kiva. Each is given an ear of white corn, which, like the ear presented at childbirth, is referred to as "mother corn." The novices receive the mother corn during the Powamuy initiation because they are about to be reborn into a spiritual mode of being.

Next, all sit around the altar, which is smoked over by the elders, after which the Powamuy elders sing several sacred songs to the

Six-Point-Cloud-People as a prayer for rain, crops, and long life. During the songs an eagle feather is tied to the top of each participant's head, perhaps to symbolize the spiritual flight they all are about to undergo. The eagle feather may also symbolize the breath or sacred spark embodied by each Hopi. A whole clump of eagle feathers sits atop the head of Tcowilawu (Muy'ingwa), who represents the totality of the spiritual substance that is refracted throughout the material forms and rhythms of the world. By contrast, each Hopi embodies only a spark of the sacred, as revealed by the lone eagle feather.

Soon Tcowilawu descends into the kiva. He has a cloud-and-rain design on his forehead, terraced cloud designs for ears, and the bundle of eagle feathers on top.[44] He carries a *poota,* a plaque made of semicircular, canvaslike leaves that are hinged in the center.[45] As he dances he opens and closes various leaves, revealing symbols of cloud, rain, and lightning. He dances around the sand mosaic, opening and closing the leaves while the Kachina and Powamuy chiefs sprinkle him with medicine water and cornmeal. When Tcowilawu finishes dancing, both chiefs give him sacred cornmeal and prayer sticks, and Tcowilawu departs, followed by a few Powamuy members. The Powamuy chief then warns the novices to reveal nothing they have seen or they will be punished severely by the kachinas.

Having undergone this rite, the initiates qualify to participate in certain aspects of future kachina dances. Powamuy initiate activities were summarized by H. R. Voth:

> Those who have gone through this initiation have in the first place become members of the Powamuy fraternity, and as such the boys and men are entitled to be present at the ceremonies and learn all the secrets of that order. They may, furthermore, act as Katsinas and later as "Father" (*naamu*) of the Katsinas, i.e., as leaders of the Katsina dances who lead the Katsinas to the plaza, prompt them with cornmeal and give them prayer offerings at the dances. The girls, and women, may put up the hair whorls of the Powamuy *Katsina-manas* for the dance of the Powamuy Katsinas . . . , sprinkle the Katsina dancers . . . and participate in the Powamuy ceremonies whenever and wherever the presence of women is proper and necessary.[46]

On the next (sixth) day, in another kiva, the initiation into the Kachina society takes place for other children; the Powamuy initiates are also required to attend. The Powamuy elders construct two sand paintings and set up all other ritual objects. The larger of the mosaics symbolizes Angwusomtaqa (Crow Mother) kachina with two Hu' (Whipper) kachinas beside her. The smaller one contains symbols of the six directions, with a Hopi "road of life" extending to the east, toward the life-giving sunrise. As Talayesva related, the smaller sand mosaic represents "the Sipapu—the opening in the earth within the Grand Canyon from which the human race emerged."[47] The *sipaapuni*, or earth navel, is the Hopi's religious center, the point from which the creation of all life and forms issued and the point to which the breath bodies of the deceased travel to return to the spiritual realm. After the mosaics are built, the village chief and the priests who assisted him during Soyalangw enter wearing their ceremonial objects, each carrying the staff symbolic of his position.

After the novices are admitted to the kiva, their ceremonial fathers and mothers sprinkle sacred cornmeal on both the large and small sand mosaics and then ask the novices to step into a ring made of four yucca leaves tied together with a hawk feather attached to each of the four knots. Two men on either side raise and lower the ring four times for each initiate, expressing the wish for a long and happy life. Then the initiates are seated on the raised (profane) floor of the kiva.

The Kachina chief and his assistant enter the kiva, bringing several trays of prayer sticks and sacred cornmeal. They stand between the ladder and the fireplace and smoke a pipe while frequently looking up as if expecting someone. Suddenly Muy'ingwa descends the ladder. He carries in his left hand a long crook symbolic of the Hopi road of life, a chief's jug, and an ancient weeding tool.[48]

After a greeting from the Kachina chief, Muy'ingwa tells the neophytes about the sacred history of the kachinas, including their arrival from the four directions, their home in the San Francisco

Mountains and other shrines, and how they brought crops to the Hopi. Muy'ingwa also teaches the initiates other fundamental sacred aspects of the Hopi way of life. He sprinkles the novices with sacred water from the chief's jug and prays that they might live to old age. Then he orders the Kachina chief to see that the novices are whipped with yucca blades to enlighten their hearts and to lead them over life's road. The whipping also reveals another homology between plant life and the Hopi mode of being. For just as the desert wind whips the tender plant stalks so that they strike their roots deeper into the earth, the ceremonial whipping helps Hopi children to strike the roots of their being deeper into the ground of the Hopi cosmos, thereby gaining a firm sense of identity and orientation.[49]

Muy'ingwa then leaves the kiva, and the Mudhead kachinas (*Kooyemsi*) come out from behind a blanket.[50] They walk four times around the sand painting that symbolizes the cosmic center and then stop, one on each side. The Mudhead on the north side picks up the corn ear and stone thereon, touches each novice with them, and returns the objects to their proper position. The same procedure is followed by the Mudheads on the east, south, and west sides, and then they all disappear behind the blanket.

An anxious silence pervades the kiva in anticipation of the Whippers. Suddenly the sound of the Whippers is heard above, amid much stomping on the kiva roof. The two Whippers and Crow Mother enter, the latter a figure of great dignity carrying several bunches of yucca blades tied at the base. They take up their positions on the north side of the kiva around the large sand painting, waving their whips, giving their calls, and jumping up and down so that their bells and rattles add to the commotion.

The ceremonial sponsors proceed to take the boys (undressed) and the girls (dressed) up to the sand painting to be given four severe lashes. The ceremonial parent may, if he or she wishes, step forward and receive two of the four lashes. When every child has been purified (whipped), the Whippers whip each other and the Crow Mother. Then the Kachina chief dismisses them with gifts of breath feathers and sacred cornmeal, and the three kachinas ascend the kiva ladder, circle the hatch four times, and depart. The

Kachina chief warns the initiates never to reveal the ceremonial secrets just seen on pain of severe punishment by the kachinas. The ceremonial sponsors then leave with their children and take them to their homes for an elaborate feast.

Fred Eggan, who, along with Mischa Titiev, participated in parts of a Powamuy performance in 1934, wrote that the Powamuy and Kachina initiations were in part concerned with instructing the Hopi youth about the sacred dimensions of crop growth. He also noted that the initiations introduced Hopi children to traditions about death. The novices learned that the ancestors were Cloud People who returned to Hopiland in the form of kachinas. Also, by participating in the initiations, a Hopi child earned the right to return to the underworld after death like an adult, since the breaths of uninitiated children who died were understood to hover around their mothers' houses awaiting rebirth.[51]

The Seventh and Eighth Days

On the seventh day little transpires. At sunrise a messenger is sent to fetch spruce (a strong prayer medium for rain) from Kisiwu, a spring that is the home of Tcowilawu. The messenger takes prayer sticks and breath feathers to deposit, a bone whistle to announce his arrival to the spirits, and a chief's jug to collect sacred spring water. Back at the kiva, ritual smoking takes place at intervals throughout the day.

Before sunrise on the eighth day, the messenger returns from Kisiwu. On entering Powamuy kiva, he gives the Powamuy chief the spruce, the chief's jug, and the bone whistle. The chief then sprinkles ashes over the messenger's head to discharm him from his contact with the sacred and administers an emetic to purify the messenger further. All wait silently until the boy finishes vomiting. Then all smoke and exchange kinship terms, and the Kachina chief sprinkles sacred meal over the returned objects to consecrate them. He next spits honey over the ritual objects and carefully rubs honey over the butts of the spruce branches and the rim of the netted chief's jug. The honey is both an offering to the kachinas and a symbol of a rich harvest through which the Hopi can concentrate their hearts in prayer. Then the messenger relates the events of his pilgrimage and the Powamuy chief prepares offerings for an afternoon ritual.

Later, another kiva member is sent to another spring (traditionally in Oraibi to the northeast) to fetch water. He takes a *pöötavi* (feather prayer path, breath feather with string attached symbolizing road of life) and eight plain breath feathers made earlier by the Powamuy chief, as well as a chief's jug, some sacred cornmeal, and a bone whistle. When he arrives at the spring he blows the whistle four times to summon the Cloud People from the four cardinal directions. He breathes a short prayer, places four breath feathers in a nearby niche, and sprinkles some meal from each of the six directions. Then he dips the chief's jug six times to further induce the clouds to bring rain, and fills the vessel with spring water. Finally, heading back toward the village, he places the feather prayer path on the trail along with the other four breath feathers and sprinkles a cornmeal path from the spring over the feather prayer path toward the village. This is a prayer that the rains will replenish the spring and then visit the village and its fields.

On his return to the kiva, the final altar ceremony takes place before the altar is dismantled. Then all that remains is the sand ridge, the standards, medicine water, and prayer sticks. An elaborate secret "discharming" rite *(naavootsiwa)* follows; it includes another song prayer to the six directions. The Hopi understand each ceremony to carry its own whip (disease), a dangerous phenomenon from which all ritual participants must be discharmed.[52]

Kachina Visitors

Early the next morning the entire village is astir well before sunrise. The bean shoots are cut, bundled, and taken to each household as presents to the young children from the kachinas.[53] These gifts are presented to the uninitiated as signs of the miraculous powers of the kachinas, who in former days "actually" lived among the Hopi. The Powamuy chief smokes over a tray containing four spruce twigs, some bean and corn sprout leaves, four eagle wing feathers, a bone whistle, a chief's jug, and four double prayer sticks.

At dawn the Soyalangw Crier chief, the village chief, and the War chief, each carrying a chief's stick, emerge from a kiva to make a morning prayer to the sun. A few moments later a sound, "Hu hu hu hu hu," is heard, and soon the Hahay'i Wuuti (Kachina Mother) appears. After dancing at a shrine, the Kachina Mother is led toward the village by a Powamuy member, who prays over "her" while leading her with a path of cornmeal. She enters the plaza, where women and children sprinkle her with cornmeal and take from her tray some corn shoots and pine sprigs. This ceremony is perhaps a prayer for fertility among Hopi women, given the association of Hahay'i Wuuti with childbirth.[54] Hahay'i Wuuti moves very slowly, perhaps as a prayer that the coming growing season will be long. Moving to the Powamuy kiva, she is blessed with smoke and medicine water by Powamuy officers, then dismissed with breath feathers and sacred cornmeal.

Meanwhile Ewtoto, the chief kachina, and Ahooli, the next in importance, emerge from Mongwi (Chief) kiva and make their way toward Hahay'i Wuuti at Powamuy kiva. Ewtoto and Ahooli both carry a chief's stick, a chief's jug, some green corn sprouts, and a bag of sacred cornmeal. Ewtoto makes a mark on the ground and Ahooli sets his staff on it, circling it while uttering a long, drawn-out cry. Titiev was told that the mark drawn by Ewtoto symbolizes the village around which Ahooli circles to indicate ultimate ownership of the village by the two kachinas.[55] Talayesva called it a "cloud symbol."[56] Perhaps this rite is both a prayer for rain to fall on the village and its fields and a commemoration of the sacred origins of each Hopi village. Indeed, the Hopi perceive a return to their origins as practically efficacious, for the world then was especially fertile and harmonious.

The two kachinas go to a hole symbolic of a cistern, into which Ewtoto deposits a prayer stick and some sacred cornmeal. He sprinkles cornmeal from the six directions and pours water into the hole from his netted jug. Ahooli repeats the prayer for rain to fill the village's cisterns, then both kachinas rejoin Hahay'i Wuuti on the east side of the kiva hatch and simultaneously pour water from the chief's jugs down the hatch to symbolize "the bringing of much rain."[57]

Next the Tobacco, Powamuy, and Kachina chiefs, along with other Powamuy officers, emerge from the kiva. The Powamuy chief carries the medicine bowl, aspergillum, a prayer stick, and some cornmeal. The Tobacco chief carries a pipe, the Kachina chief a prayer stick and some cornmeal, and the rest cornmeal and breath feathers. The Tobacco chief blows smoke over the three kachinas. The Powamuy chief sprinkles them with medicine water and gives them the prayer stick and cornmeal in exchange for Hahay'i Wuuti's tray of corn and bean shoots. The Kachina chief gives them the prayer stick and cornmeal, and the rest give them the cornmeal and breath feathers.

Ewtoto and Ahooli then visit several important households, including the Bear and Piikyas clan houses, where they repeat the rite of drawing and circling a cloud symbol. Ewtoto draws four cornmeal lines on the houses and gives the senior clan woman a bunch of corn sprouts. Then they are dismissed, and so is Hahay'i Wuuti. All go to a kachina shrine southeast of the village to deposit their offerings.

Feasts are held the rest of the day, and in the afternoon a great many kachinas are seen wandering the streets, presenting gifts to the children. Though there is no formal organization to their appearance, the kachinas are generally led by Hee'e'e, the Warrior Mother. Traditionally on this day on Third Mesa, the Giant Kachinas (So'yoko) were seen making their rounds and threatening to carry off misbehaving children, who would be ransomed for generous amounts of food by their families. But the So'yoko ceremony became detached from the Powamuya ceremony on Third Mesa sometime before 1934.

Introduction to Symbolism

Late in the evening, final preparations are made for the Bean Dance. About midnight, after the kachina dancers leave their respective kivas to go to a shrine to pray, the initiates are brought into the kivas. The kachinas then return to their kivas, where they perform a night dance. The neophytes are seated on the east bench with their knees drawn up to their chins, symbolizing their child-like status. The kachinas announce their arrival and again descend into their kivas. This time they wear no "friends" (masks), and for the first time the novices realize that the kachinas, whom they imagined to be actual deities, are their own living relatives. As Titiev noted, "In such dramatic fashion is the most important of all kachina secrets revealed to Hopi children."[58]

Numerous written accounts by Hopis have described the initial shock, disappointment, and anger experienced by the neophytes when the unmasked kachinas appear.[59] Then how could this new experience be "the most important of all kachina secrets"? Aren't the Hopi children learning that the kachinas are only human impersonations? The answer, I think, is no. For the Hopi, we must not forget, all of reality has both a spiritual and a material dimension; the spiritual reveals itself through the material, and the material occasions the experience of the spiritual. This fundamental aspect of Hopi religiosity is realized during, or more probably after, the Hopi Bean Dance. Reality is paradoxical; that is, it is not one dimensional, as children think it is. Hopi children think that humans are simply human (profane) and that kachinas are simply gods (sacred). From the Bean Dance they learn that reality is not always what it appears to be at first glance. The kachinas, whom they had always experienced in a naive manner as sacred, are revealed to be human impersonations; but the lesson cuts two ways, for later (Titiev says after one or two years) the initiates realize that what appears at first as profane may actually embody the sacred. As Emory Sekaquaptewa noted, "When it is revealed to him that the kachina is just an impersonation, an impersonation which possesses a spiritual essence, the child's security is not destroyed. Instead, the experience strengthens the individual in another phase of his life in the community."[60] Sam Gill argued that whereas the uninitiated see only the material form of the kachinas, the initiated see spirit in matter—indeed, that the sacred can only reveal itself through some material phenomenon, for the spiritual as such remains unmanifest.[61]

Kachinas are not perceived by Hopis as impersonations following the Bean Dance, or at least not simply as impersonations. The Hopi who dances the kachina does remain himself, but he is simultaneously the spiritual being he seeks to reveal. Emory Seka- quaptewa and Don Talayesva have both written that a Hopi actual- ly becomes the kachina he dances, and thus kachina ceremonies remain very solemn and important prayers for rain and life itself.[62]

Hopi oral traditions relate that the "real" kachinas once fre- quented the mesas but departed.[63] Before leaving they gave the Hopi masks and taught them how to dance the masks in order to embody the sacred essence of the kachinas. By repeating the direc- tions of the kachinas as laid down in the "ancient time ago," the Hopi are able to project themselves into the realm of the sacred in a participatory manner.

The Bean Dance

In the Bean Dance, each group of dancers begins in its own kiva and then travels to the others twice, finishing the round of dances in their own kiva. During an intermission between dances, many gifts are exchanged between the men and the women, and it is often during this time that a girl will offer her sweetheart a loaf of sweet cornmeal (qomi) as a marriage proposal. The dances last through the night, and the novices are allowed to watch them for the first time, although they still must sit with knees drawn up, like an embryo in the womb.

When the performance is over, the initiates are warned to tell no one about what they have seen or they will be punished severely by the Whippers. The initiates are then taken to the homes of their ceremonial aunts, where their heads are washed (purified) with yucca suds, after which they receive new names. Meanwhile the Bean Dancers remove their corn husk squash blossom headdresses and place them in a shrine or plant them in a field as a prayer for rain.[64]

The Bean Dance ordinarily concludes Powamuya except for the customary four-day period of ritual abstinence from sex, salt, and meat. However, when Wuwtsim initiations were held, Powamuya was extended by the Patsavu rite, which was performed the day following the Kachina initiations. Hee'e'e Kachina led a procession of kachinas through the village in a reenactment of the primordial migrations of the Badger clan and the kachinas.

Theoretical Reflections

H. R. Voth's description of the Oraibi Powamuya ceremony remains the most complete account of this important ritual. His basic interpretation of the rite was that it symbolizes preparing the fields "for the approaching season."[65] But Titiev's interpretation is perhaps more to the point. According to Titiev, Powamuya "is a ritual designed to promote fertility and germination."[66] Bradfield echoed and elaborated that point when he stated that Powamuya's purpose is to "promote the germination and early growth of the seeds to be planted in the fields a few weeks later."[67] Talayesva felt that by virtue of the Powamuya ritual, "we had secured ourselves against crop failure." He also noted the practical significance of the rite: "I saw the importance of the Powamuy ceremony for successful farming. The old people praised my work and said that when this ceremony was not performed correctly famines occurred."[68]

The primary purpose of Powamuya therefore seems to be to bring about warm weather and more precipitation in order to prepare the fields for planting in the spring, the success of the harvest being "ritually planned" by the success of the bean and corn shoot harvests. This meaning is most explicitly revealed by the germination and growth of corn and bean sprouts in the heated kivas following the arrival of the blackbird, a harbinger of warm weather, and by the appearance of various kachinas. The Hopi kachinas dance from roughly December until July (from Soyalangw through the Home Dance), that is, essentially from the winter solstice through the summer solstice. Kachina ceremonies are thus linked with warm weather as well as with the pervasive concerns for moisture, health, and fertility.

Closely related to this meaning is Powamuya's connection with the Kachina cult itself as demonstrated in the Powamuy and Kachina initiation rituals. All initiates are qualified to dance in future kachina rites, and those inducted into the Powamuy society earn the potential privilege of serving as "fathers" of the kachinas.

Underlying these rights and privileges is the ceremonial knowledge related to the growth of plants and the even more fundamental lesson that material and spiritual realms are inseparable.

The Powamuya rites also reenact a great deal of Hopi mythology, especially of the Badger clan, which "owns" the ceremony. Tcowilawu and Muy'ingwa, both ancestors to the Badger clan, relate the Badger clan and kachina mythology to the Powamuy and Kachina initiates respectively. Indeed, during the Patsavu rite the mythology of the kachinas and the Badger clan is "relived," thus reactualizing the "long ago" when the rite was first performed.

The practical and religious concerns of Powamuya should be apparent from the preceding interpretation. Similar concerns could be easily revealed in a discussion of the other rites of the Hopi. It is, however, important to note that Powamuya is practically significant because it was first conducted in the "long ago" by the mythical ancestors. The Hopi feel that they can affect the cosmos in a practical manner, but only by returning to the beginning through techniques taught by their ancestors. It is quite fair to say, as I stated earlier, that the Hopi experience of the sacred is intrinsically linked with practical life-giving matters. But it is precisely this relationship that many previous investigators have failed to spell out concretely.

As Kennard and Titiev noted years ago, one of the most fundamental aspects of Hopi religion is the perception of the continuity of life and death.[69] This relationship between life and death is truly inseparable, and thus the Hopi have no separate rituals for these aspects of the cosmos (except, of course, for birth and funeral rites). The Hopi pray for rain, crops, and health to the kachinas, who are, in one sense, departed Hopi ancestors. The Hopi offer their ancestors gifts (smoke, prayer sticks, breath feathers, sacred cornmeal) in exchange for the gift of life, which the ancestors imparted to their descendants. The two worlds, the afterlife and the here and now, are inseparable in Hopi eyes. In fact, one of the last things spoken to a deceased Hopi at his or her funeral is a plea to return soon to the village as a cloud person to bless the living with the spiritual substance.

Furthermore, the Hopi overcome the distance between themselves and their ancestors through the repetition of actions laid down in the "long ago" by their ancestors. In Powamuya the Hopi feel that they are performing the ritual not only *as* it was originally performed but *when* it was originally performed. In this sense they overcome the problem of death (time) by symbolically reactualizing the timeless time when Powamuya originated. In essence, they become their ancestors, an experience that is commemorative and therefore practical. The commemorative aspects of Hopi ritual are unquestionably transcendent, having reference to the origin, nature, and destiny of the world. For that very reason they are practically and physically important, a point not realized even by some of the most recent scholars of Hopi religion.[70]

Finally, the practicality of Hopi prayer rites not only presupposes religious experience; it also occasions religious experience. The practical expression of Hopi ceremonies embodies fundamental religious significance, since the Hopi experience the sacred through the concrete forms and rhythms of their world. The concrete practicality of their world manifests itself as sacred, for it is the sacred that creates and sustains the world's life and forms. To perceive and live in the world is to experience the "very something" upon which it is constituted. Hopi ceremonialism yields life, and life evokes religion.

The Hopi understanding of prayer may well operate on two levels of meaning simultaneously: the existential and the cosmic. Here Mircea Eliade's division of sacred mythic time into the first and second primordia is helpful. His first primordium refers to a precosmic, unhistorical, speculative level inaccessible to human beings, while his second primordium refers to a cosmogonic, historical, existential level when human life was created.[71]

Both levels are evident in Hopi mythology. The first primordium is the time during which the Hopi gestated in the womb of the earth, before their emergence through the earth navel to this world. The second primordium is the sacred history that transpired with the emergence, the migrations, and the settlement of the villages; it ended with the departure of the kachinas, which marked the end of the mythic era. Once the kachinas departed, the Hopi acquired symbolic religious experience. This experience, of course, became fundamental to their religious orientation, as demonstrated by the Powamuy and Kachina initiations. It was then that the Hopi became human, in the full sense of the word. Hopi experiences of the "long ago" generally involve both levels, but from time to time one level may be emphasized more than the other. Both periods form one sacred time, and both are equally important to the Hopi.

Both levels are found in the two modalities of Hopi religion, the practical and the ceremonial. Farming, for example, recalls the second primordium, the "time" of the ancestors who first planted seeds and cared for their plants. But farming also evokes the experience of the first primordium through the myth that connects the emergence of Hopis with plants. It may be true that the first primordium is prior to the appearance of humans in the strict sense, but it is important to remember that Hopi religious experience relates humans to almost all cosmic forms and rhythms. Thus they, or at least that aspect of humans that is constitutive of everything—breath—can experience the first primordium, the totality that existed before their emergence.

The same twofold structure is evident in Hopi rites of passage. The Hopi mother kneels over a bed of sand to deliver her child. Her action is symbolic of the first Hopi mother, who is said to have delivered her child thusly.[72] Yet the bed of sand also symbolizes the earth mother, from whose womb all life emerged in the beginning. In the latter meaning, the pregnant woman is likened to Tuwapongtumsi, who gave birth to all life and forms. Marriage rites are similar. They are based on the rites of the first Hopi couple, but they also symbolize the primordial union of Sootukwnangw (Heaven) and Tuwapongtumsi, from which came the fertilizing fluid of creation.[73]

Even death recalls the first primordium. That may seem odd at first, given that death did not occur until after the Hopi had emerged to this world. But death is perceived as a reactualization of the spiritual, precosmic totality. At death the breath returns to its origin, the womb of the earth, from which all future life forms emerge.

The twofold structure of Hopi myth is also revealed in all formal ceremonies. It can be readily seen that Powamuya, for one, reenacts both primordia. The arrival of the kachinas and the Badger clan (second primordium) is reenacted during Powamuya; but so is the emergence, at least implicitly, by virtue of the fact that most of this rite (and of others as well) is performed in the kivas, which are underground ceremonial chambers with four levels, each of which corresponds to one of the four worlds of the emergence. To exit from the kiva to the surface is a symbolic reenactment of the emergence itself, so that Powamuya also embodies the experience of the first primordium.

The physical nature of the Powamuya ceremonies evokes the religious experience of the beginning, which is significant practically, at both the cosmic and the specifically human levels. At the same time, these ceremonies—and the others celebrated in Hopiland—produce life, through which the sacred is experienced. Thus there are two separate but related modes by which the Hopi experience the "very something" that is ultimate reality. One way is active, the other passive. But these modes are not fractured in Hopi religious life. Both modes are embodied within each significant Hopi experience, though one or the other is generally emphasized or expressed. Work and ritual, practice and religion, activity and passivity are inextricably intertwined, a connection with which our method of interpretation should be consistent.

Part II

Dominance and Religion

Four

Contact and Change

Having delved into the basic aspects of traditional Hopi religion, it might be tempting at this point to end this investigation. But to do so would be premature, because it remains to be seen how the Hopi are coming to terms religiously with the problems they confront in the contemporary world. The Hopi unquestionably have undergone considerable change owing to the influence of the dominant non-Hopi culture. Virtually all significant aspects of Hopi life and hence of Hopi religion have been influenced by the European and American invasions of their land and their lives.

Change for the Hopi is nothing new, of course. They have known many changes since their emergence to this world, as clan histories relate. But have all these changes been essentially of the same type? The answer is not simple.

When I first began to examine the kinds of change undergone by the Hopi I felt that three modes needed to be distinguished: internal, unforced external, and forced external change. Internal change refers to transitions that involve only the Hopi people and the natural environment from which they receive their life and religion. Unforced external change results from relatively peaceful contact and exchange with other peoples. The third type, forced external change, refers to the past century of white domination.

Archaeological studies suggest that sometime between A.D. 500 and 700 Hopi life changed from meandering to sedentary. Hopi traditions say that the settlement of their present lands occurred when they arrived at a place that revealed itself as the center of the world. The exact nature of the revelation varies. A number of

Hopis from First Mesa say that their mesa was settled because it contained a certain yellow flower as foretold by the gods in the underworld. Some Hopis from Second and Third Mesas say that the Hopi began settling the mesas when a prophesied bright star lit up the sky.[1] Despite the differences in these myths, it is clear the Hopi feel that they settled their present lands according to their own dynamics. They deciphered a message from the cosmos that struck them as auspicious and sacred according to ancient prophecy.

That kind of change should be distinguished from change that involves relatively peaceful contact and exchange with other peoples. I am thinking, for instance, of the origin of the Hopi's maize agriculture. Several Hopi myths tell how the supernatural kachinas brought crops to the Hopi from the four directions, especially from the south and the underworld. One initiated Third Mesa Hopi told me that "underworld" points to a South American origin for corn. Other Hopis have implied that the Hopi emergence myth is symbolic, not historical, and expresses the Hopis' close relationship with their world. Either way, it is clear that the Hopi recognize an external origin for the introduction of corn, and they are supported by linguistic and archaeological evidence.

Perhaps a simpler example of externally directed but peaceful change is the introduction of machine-woven cloth, canned goods, and metalware during the nineteenth century, when the Hopi had relatively peaceful contacts with white Americans and willingly adopted some of their material cultural items. These early exchanges apparently were not forced by the whites. Still another example is the Hopi's borrowing of dances from the Zuni, the Navajo, and the Comanche. The Hopi, according to some traditions, even received and incorporated a number of members from other tribes, including the Apache, Paiute, and Pima.[2] In historical times they received the Tewa from the Rio Grande Pueblos.

Internal and unforced external changes continue to take place in the twentieth century, but a new type, forced change based on political power, has been added. Though the Spanish overpowered the Hopi for 140 years (from 1540 to 1680), they had no significant influence. They did introduce sheepherding and peach orchards, but the Hopi never used the horse much, and the Spanish seem to have had little effect on Hopi religious practices. The Hopi were finally able to free themselves from Spanish rule owing to their conservative nature and their geographical isolation. With the coming of white Americans, however, the Hopi faced an adversary who would not be turned back, and Hopi consciousness clearly differentiates the episodic character of the limited Spanish rule and the dominance by white Americans whose numbers and strength seem insurmountable.[3]

The Hopi have had disputes with various Native American peoples over the centuries, but these conflicts were different from the problems posed by white Americans. Even the Navajo, a fierce and long-time enemy of the Hopi, have not denied the Hopi a sense of humanity or religious authenticity, recognizing that Hopis have a sophisticated and practical religious orientation to the world and not attempting to change their manner of life.

Whites, however, have for the most part perceived the Hopi as "primitive," as somewhat less than human, and have attempted to forcibly change the Hopi way of being in terms of their own "civilized" cultural patterns. Furthermore, Hopi religion, if recognized at all, has been perceived by whites as crude or demonic, and attempts have been made to convert the Hopi to various forms of Christianity. The Hopi themselves recognize the qualitative and quantitative changes they have experienced since the late nineteenth century, and I have been told by several Hopis, both young and old, that their biggest problem today is trying to come to terms with the rapid changes forced upon them by the dominant society.

In discussing these three modes of changes with Emory Sekaquaptewa, I gained an important insight on the Hopi's understanding of religion and modernity. Sekaquaptewa told me that my morphology of changes was essentially accurate on one level but was incomplete. While it was true, he said, that the Hopi perceived the forced changes of the twentieth century as different from those of former times, they simultaneously perceived them as fulfilling prophecies (navoti) foretold in the beginning. On one hand, the losses were resented and lamented, but on the other hand, they foretold the coming of a purification day, when the corruption of the world would be removed.[4] Thus, to the degree that contemporary Hopi cultural change is experienced as instituted by humans, it is viewed with a sense of loss and of spiritual impurity. If such changes are understood within the context of continuity based on prophecy, however, they are accepted as sacred and meaningful. The loss of one mythic tradition is replaced by the remembrance of another timeless pattern—and that occasions an experience of spiritual solace.

This interpretation of the Hopi experience of twentieth-century cultural change seems to illuminate the understanding by the Hopi of their own historical vicissitudes at a general level. Furthermore, such a method is able to shed light on the Hopi experience of different types of cultural change, because all Hopi cultural change is first appropriated through the paradox I have been discussing. Such theoretical abstractions are of little value, however, when separated so artificially from their historical context. It is time to look more closely at the web of events that constitute Hopi twentieth-century cultural contact and change.

Early Contacts with Whites

The first significant Hopi contact with a white American came in 1862. The Mormon missionary Jacob Hamblin arrived at Oraibi that year and helped form a Hopi settlement at Moencopi, where the Hopi had farmed for centuries.[5] Hamblin not only introduced new cultigens, such as turban squash, safflower, and sorghum; he also planted the seeds of Mormonism.[6]

The Mormon faith, though accepted by only a few Hopis, has been more successful than any other missionary movement among the Hopi. Mormonism holds that all Native Americans are descendants of the evil Lamanites, one of the original twelve tribes of Israel. Various Native American gods are said to be versions of Jesus, who the Mormons believe visited the New World after leaving the Old World. Though this Mormon tradition is rejected by many Hopis as inaccurate,[7] it appears to harmonize with the Hopi understanding, especially prevalent on Third Mesa, that the

Hopi migrated to the New World from the Old World in the "long ago." Some Hopis have told me, for instance, that the original *sipaapuni* (earth navel) was in Egypt, India, or Jerusalem—that is, somewhere in the Old World.[8]

In the century since Hamblin's missionary efforts, Mormons have, as a whole, been quite tolerant of traditional Hopi religious patterns. Hopis who convert to the Mormon faith rarely if ever renounce their Hopi religious background, for the Mormon faith accepted by most Hopis is intertwined with their older religious patterns. Most Mormon Hopis see no problem with being both Hopi and Mormon, and those who drop Hopi ritual do so because it was prophesied that they should. Helen Sekaquaptewa's father once told her this prophecy:

> There will come a time when the written record will be brought to the Hopis by the white man. There will be many religions taught. You will need to be wise to recognize and choose the right church. It will teach you to be humble and will not try to force you into it. When that time comes we should all forsake our native religion and join this true church. There will come a time when all the people of the earth will belong to the one true church, we will all speak the same language and be as one people.[9]

Sekaquaptewa said that her father told her this prophecy before she had ever heard of the Book of Mormon. When she saw the book, it seemed to echo many Hopi traditions, and Mormon seemed to be the religion her father had foretold. The Hopi rules of proper behavior also seemed similar to the Ten Commandments. Eventually she became Mormon.[10] Interestingly, then, the new church her father prophesied ultimately fulfills the teachings of the Hopi religious tradition.

John Wesley Powell, the first white man to explore the Colorado River, was guided by Hamblin to Oraibi in 1870. He found the Hopi to be quite friendly and lived among them harmoniously for several weeks. He had great respect for Hopi religious traditions, and after a while he gained the trust of many Hopis. Because of that trust he was admitted to a kiva during an important ceremony and recorded this prayer to Muy'ingwa:

Muingwa pash lolomai, Master of the Clouds, we eat no stolen bread; our young men ride not the stolen ass; our food is not stolen from the gardens of our neighbors. Muingwa pash lolomai, we beseech of thee to dip your great sprinkler, made of the feathers of the birds of the heavens, into the lakes of the skies and sprinkle us with sweet rains, that the ground may be prepared in the winter for the corn that grows in the summer.[11]

Upon his return to Washington, Powell proved to be of practical benefit to the Hopi, successfully fighting Indian Bureau plans that would have hurt the Hopi. Thus Powell's visits, like Hamblin's, were friendly. But matters soon changed.

The White Traders

Between 1870 and 1910 white traders confronted the Hopi.[12] Thomas Keams established a trading post east of Walpi in 1875, and by 1910 seven traders were located on Hopi lands.[13] Four were Hopi, and the other three were licensed white traders. The main goods the traders introduced to the Hopi were canned goods, coffee, kettles, axes, pickaxes, spades, and woven cloth.[14] By the 1890s, Hopis widely used metal tools and woven cloth; further-more, pane glass windows began to replace selenite window panes, and doors to houses were placed in the walls rather than on the roofs.[15]

Unfortunately, few data were gathered during this initial period of material cultural change in terms of possible correlative changes in the religious consciousness of the Hopi. Given the religious dimension of Hopi material culture and practice, it is reasonable to assume that the widespread replacement of stone tools with metal tools and hand-spun cloth with machine-woven cloth might evoke some type of examination and reflection, if nothing else, at the religious level. Of course, different Hopis may have per-ceived the changes differently, depending especially on their age, sex, clan heritage, ceremonial position, and village and mesa residency.

A detailed demographic study of Hopi responses to this new trade is now impossible, but my conversations with Hopis suggest that the introduction of metal wares, woven cloth, and canned goods may have received little attention initially. Hopi oral tradition relates that when all peoples emerged from the earth navel in the beginning, a white brother emerged with the Hopi and migrated toward the east. The white brother was said to possess great knowledge and was to return one day to the Hopi, bringing many benefits.[16] Religiously, the arrival of the white Americans and their superior technology may have been viewed at first as the fulfillment of Hopi prophecy. This seems plausible, given the almost universal acceptance by Hopi of certain European material goods.

Whether viewed as simply an exchange between peoples or as the fulfillment of a prophecy, the Hopi and white Americans enjoyed peaceful and fruitful relationships at first. The Hopi were able to choose the offerings of the whites at their own pace, without pressure. They willingly accepted the goods but did not quickly become dependent on them. Indeed, to this day many Hopi take pride in saying that they could still subsist if tomorrow they lost all Western technological influence.

Directed Cultural Change

The United States government began making formal contacts with the Hopi after 1870, when Indian agents began visiting. Despite Powell's efforts, the majority of late nineteenth-century government officials perceived the Hopi as "primitives" whose ways were inferior to the "civilized" manners of their own culture. As Harry James, a historian of Hopi, noted, the Indian agents were quite intolerant of Hopi religious traditions and were "dedicated to do everything within their power to make the Hopi into an imitation and second-class white man, rather than the best type of Hopi citizen."[17]

Unlike the Spanish, the United States agents would not be turned away, and the expanding nation's sheer size and power forced the Hopi to deal with them. The United States did not simply offer the Hopi a few material items; it confronted the Hopi directly in a way that affected the very being of the Hopi. From

1870 on, the Hopi have been confronted with a fundamental and crucial problem: how can the Hopi satisfy the demands of the dominant society and yet maintain some sense of Hopi authenticity and self-determination? The United States government, from 1870 to 1934, made a strong effort to "convert and civilize" the Hopi, who tried to resist such conquest without being exterminated by a superior political force.

In 1882, for instance, the commissioner of Indian affairs issued a map of the Hopi Reservation as determined by President Chester A. Arthur.[18] It greatly reduced Hopi land holdings. The Hopi were never consulted prior to President Arthur's decision, and they knew little or nothing about reading U.S. government maps. Their land has always been determined by various shrines and topographical features around the junction of the San Juan River with the Colorado to the north, the Arizona–New Mexico border on the east, the Mogollon and Zuni rim on the south, and the San Francisco Mountains on the west.[19] Indeed, some Hopis claim that the Spanish gave the Hopi a land grant that recognized their traditional boundaries, and a search has been undertaken to find it.[20] Since Hopi religion sustained the Hopi and since Hopi religion was bound up inextricably with their land, they could not accept an arbitrarily conceived reservation that omitted many important places. Therefore, it is understandable that after 1882 relations between the Hopi and the federal government began to deteriorate rapidly.

At the same time Navajo encroachments on Hopi lands escalated, so that Lololoma, village chief of Oraibi, along with several other chiefs, went to Washington with Thomas Keams, the white trader who had befriended the Hopi.[21] The Hopi told the United States president of their problem with the Navajo, and the president suggested that they descend from the mesas and spread out over the valley floor in order to check the spread of the Navajo. Lololoma liked the idea and indeed was so impressed with his Washington trip that he agreed to convince his people to attend government school. It is thought that he also agreed to the establishment of a Christian mission at Oraibi.[22]

Upon his return to Oraibi, Lololoma was severely criticized by a large faction of conservative Hopis who did not want to send their children to a white school. Lololoma apparently felt for a short time that the true white brother had returned from the east as prophesied and that the Hopi should learn from their long lost brother.[23] The conservatives felt that the white Americans were not the prophesied whites because they spoke no Hopi and did not possess the other half of a stone tablet that was broken in two after the emergence, when the white brother migrated east.[24] Thus the Hopi began to experience divisions among themselves. When Frank Cushing, the ethnologist, arrived at Oraibi in 1883, he found the Hopi of that village divided into two factions.[25] One stood behind Lololoma, leader of the Bear clan, the other behind Lomahongyoma, leader of the Spider clan.

In 1887 a government school was opened in Keam's Canyon, and the government set quotas for attendance from each village. Oraibi sent few children, since the conservative faction was largest there, so troops were sent in to arrest the leaders of the resisters. The arrest of a couple of conservatives angered the remaining conservatives all the more, and they trapped Lololoma in a kiva, from which he was rescued by U.S. troops.

In 1891 the U.S. government sent surveyors to the Hopi to divide their lands among individual Hopis as prescribed by the Dawes Act of 1887.[26] The government felt that all Native Americans would hasten more quickly down the road to civilization if they were introduced to private ownership of land, the backbone of bourgeois society. Hopi lands were owned by clans, not individuals, according to tradition, and thus Hopis completely rejected the attempt to implement the Dawes Act. All Hopis, including Lololoma and his followers, objected to the attempt to divide their lands, and many children were now encouraged to leave the school at Keam's Canyon and return home. Surveyors' stakes were pulled up as soon as the surveyors left the scene. These actions led to the issuing of an order in 1891 to arrest several outspoken chiefs at Oraibi, clearly the most rebellious village.

On June 21, 1891, a small party of U.S. Cavalry approached Oraibi and arrested a few men at the base of the mesa.[27] As they entered the village, however, they were met by a large contingent of warriors, including impersonators of Spider Woman, the war gods, and Maasaw. The cavalry wisely retreated but returned on July 16 in much larger numbers. Several Hopis, including Lololoma, were arrested and taken prisoner to Fort Wingate.

By the end of the summer the two factions were completely split, with the conservatives looking to Lomahongyoma as their leader.[28] Lomahongyoma attracted the larger following and soon began to quarrel with Lololoma over the right to be village chief. Lomahongyoma said that Spider Woman had promised Oraibi to the Spider clan before they left Kawestima and migrated to Oraibi. Lololoma refuted those claims, citing an ancient tradition holding that the village chief should be of the Bear clan.

Tensions between the factions were exacerbated by the government's continued attempt to send all Hopi children to school in Keam's Canyon.[29] The conservatives resisted the increased efforts of the United States to educate their children and by 1894 were labeled "hostiles" for not cooperating. Those who agreed to send their children to the school at Keam's Canyon were labeled "friendlies." Again troops were sent in to Oraibi, and several male hostiles were rounded up and sent to Alcatraz prison for one year.

Both factions were now so bitter that they would not cooperate to perform the traditional ceremonies, a very serious problem given the importance of performing the ceremonies with a "good heart."[30] The entire ceremonial cycle was affected, for neither side would let the other use its sacred objects. Eventually Lomahongyoma took another step toward becoming the village chief and started his own Soyalangw rite, a rite traditionally led by the Bear clan head. In 1897 there were two Soyalangw festivals, and each male resident had to decide in which one he would participate. By his decision he clearly affiliated himself with one of the factions, and thus the 1897 Soyalangw ceremony demarcated the Oraibi divisions.

In addition to these problems, there were violent disputes with Navajos over land boundaries.[31] A smallpox epidemic in 1897–98 killed many Hopis, and much of the Oraibi valley soil was being eroded by an annually increasing arroyo that severely limited the amount of available farm land.[32]

A great deal of prophecy emerged at this time concerning the preordained character of the internal dispute. Tradition holds that tensions between the Bear and Spider (and Fire) clans have existed since "long ago," even though these clans are of the same phratry. Lololoma told Mischa Titiev an emergence story that attributed death and witchcraft to Spider Woman, ancestor of the Spider clan.[33] In so doing, he implicitly associated the Spider clan members with the origin of death and witchcraft, an association that, surprisingly, some Spider clan members accepted.[34] Other versions of the emergence myth blame the origin of witchcraft on the nephew of Matsito, head of the Bear clan.[35] The Bear clan claims that it has the right to lead the Hopi, for Maasaw decided when they first reached Oraibi in the "long ago" that they should be chief of all clans. The Fire clan also claims that it should lead because clan members have one-half of a stone tablet created by Spider Woman, the other half being in the hands of the true white brother.[36] Indeed, one reason the hostiles refused to acknowledge the white Americans as the true white brother was that no American had produced the other half of the tablet. The Fire clan also claims the right to lead by virtue of its relationship with Maasaw, who is their clan ancestor.[37] Clan members essentially argue that since Maasaw is the owner of Hopiland and is their ancestor, they should be in charge of the village chieftainship. As a result of these tensions, which the Hopi perceive as aboriginal, many prophecies emerged in Oraibi warning of a split of the village. Each side faulted the other, but both sides agreed that the split was prophesied from the beginning.

The Split of Oraibi

In 1906 the friendlies, led by Lololoma, and the hostiles, led by Yukioma of the Fire clan, became so at odds with each other that each faction held its own Home Dance ceremony.[38] Each side finally agreed to a pushing match to see who would leave Oraibi and form a new settlement. The friendlies won, and so the hostiles—half of the village—left Oraibi and settled Hotevilla, which was named after a slope of juniper trees overlooking a spring.[39]

Thus it appeared to many observers that the tensions inherent in the Hopi clan system led to the breakup of what was perhaps the oldest continuously inhabited village in the New World.

Some Hopis hold a different view of the split. Emory Sekaquaptewa, from Third Mesa, wrote that the "more sophisticated view is that the division itself was the substance of the prophecy, in that it was designed in deliberation or, in Hopi terms, [t]iingavi."[40] In other words, the split of Oraibi was a deliberate act.[41] According to Sekaquaptewa, "such a division was necessary to the survival of the Hopis as a people."[42] The Navajo, it will be recalled, were rapidly encroaching on Hopi lands by 1906, and the Oraibi wash was becoming a larger and larger arroyo. Furthermore, as Sekaquaptewa wrote, Oraibi had become quite large and its ceremonies were becoming profaned.[43] The Hopi needed a new village, so the chiefs got together and made a plan toward the realization of that need. The event was discussed in terms of clan frictions because the clan is the fundamental unit of the social order. Above all, clans are considered timeless and that which is timeless is real. Hopi clans provided a language through which a needed village split could be understood as meaningful religiously. And functionally, the tension between allegiance to clan and allegiance to village provided a spark that helped bring about the split.

John Bennett suggested in the 1930s that interpretations of Hopi life by the Hopi and other Pueblo peoples fall into two opposing categories: "Apollonian," which views Hopi life as extremely well integrated and cohesive, and "maladjusted," which sees Hopi life as divisive and full of friction. Bennett proposed that the difference in the two perspectives could "be resolved into one of means and ends."[44] He argued that the harmonious view of Hopi life was true of the "end," that is, the final result, but that the maladjusted view was true of the "means" used to actualize the "end." I think it is true that the divisive character of the Hopi clan system ensures the harmony of the Hopi people in the end. The very harsh semiarid environment that the Hopi live in demands that communities stay small and hearts pure. The Hopi would break their covenant with Maasaw if they were to exploit their environment indiscriminately and wastefully. Most important for the Hopi is the effect of a large village on the hearts of the people. It seems as though the Hopi way of life traditionally prevented the development of urban environments that might occasion a diminishing awareness of the dependency the Hopi have on the sacred. The history of religions reveals that the development of cities is often correlative with both a decline in religious awareness and a greater emphasis on human autonomy. Such a decline would be especially disastrous for the Hopi, who feel that their religious ceremonies are important practically for obtaining the gift of life itself.

Even the problems related to federal government interference that divided Oraibi residents into two camps embody religious dimensions. White Americans forced the Hopi to face some very difficult problems and challenged their traditional way of life in a new way. While the Spanish were repelled, the white Americans were not and thus the Hopi had to come to terms with a dominant society. It is important to remember that the Hopi thought they must maintain "good hearts" in order to communicate fruitfully with the sacred and bring rain to their parched land. Whites, by forcing Hopi children to attend schools far from the reservation, disrupted traditional Hopi modes of orientation and made the embodiment of happy hearts difficult. Under pressures from the whites to become Christianized and Westernized, Hopis found keeping good thoughts a problem, and thus they began to worry about the possibility of drought.

The Hopi were faced with a life-threatening paradox. On one hand, they felt they had to maintain their traditions to bring forth rain and fertility. On the other hand, they could do so only by refusing to cooperate with a clearly dominant society. To resist the influence of a dominant society in itself evoked many bad thoughts that the Hopi felt might spoil the ceremonies.[45] The Hopi sensed they could not simply yield to the desires of the white Americans and extinguish their traditions, yet they simultaneously felt they must resist forced change in a way that maintained good thoughts. Both the friendlies and the hostiles felt they could not survive if they did not offer prayers properly. The friendlies felt they could preserve "good hearts" only if they cooperated with the powerful whites by sending their children to school. The hostiles felt that "good hearts" could not be maintained if many basic Hopi traditions were lost, and thus they resisted government influence more directly than did the friendlies. Both factions represented responses to modernity that attempted to preserve the religious character of the Hopi. In that sense, the two groups were serving similar ends. Perhaps their factionalism symbolized the end of the aboriginal Hopi way in response to white American dominance.[46]

The situation in 1906 was complicated further by prophetic understandings of modernity. I mentioned earlier the ambivalence experienced by contemporary Hopis as they attempt to come to terms with modernity. On one hand, Hopis perceived the dominant influence of the white Americans as a phenomenon which they must try to resist; on the other hand, they saw it as an unavoidable, prophesied change. Hopi prophecy held that Spider clan members would one day return north to Kawestima, their ancestral home, from which they had migrated to Oraibi.[47] For unknown reasons the hostiles never migrated all the way to Kawestima, but the return there was cited by all Hopis concerned as prophesied since the mythic era.[48] At the same time, another prophecy asserted that if the Hopi acquiesced to the white Americans, Paalölöqangw, the great water serpent of the underworld, would roll over and destroy the world by flood.[49] Indeed, Yukioma, leader of the hostiles, told the Indian agent Leo Crane that it was for everyone's good that the hostiles preserved the Hopi way.

Prophecy also surrounded the friendlies. One prophecy pronounced that ceremonialism at Oraibi would one day end.[50] To placate the U.S. government, Tawaquaptewa, who succeeded Lololoma as village chief of Oraibi in 1901 or 1902, went away to the Sherman Institute in California after the split of Oraibi.[51] At a time when he hardly understood English, he was duped into signing a statement, contrary to his convictions, that the Hopi in Oraibi should cooperate fully with the government. When he finally returned to Oraibi in the summer of 1909, he was bitter yet resigned about the rift in his village. He was also disturbed to find a group of hostiles there in residence. Though Oraibi had split three years earlier to end the ceremonial cycle, Tawaquaptewa decided to have the Wuwtsim initiation in November and wanted the hostiles out of Oraibi before that time.[52] An argument was planned by Tawaquaptewa and Kewanimptewa to create friction between the two factions sufficient to evoke a migration. All went according to plan, and Kewanimptewa led his faction out of Oraibi and formed the village of Bacavi. Furthermore, numerous Oraibis had taken up many of the ways of the whites and had even adopted Christianity. This infuriated Tawaquaptewa, who said all converts must leave, and a migration of Christian Hopis from Oraibi established the village of Kikotsmovi. Tawaquaptewa sent other Hopis, who were very poor, to Moencopi to farm.[53]

Seeing his village disintegrate before his eyes, Tawaquaptewa became even more bitter, yet resigned to a prophetic understanding of the change. Some Hopis say that when he died he was buried in his Ewtoto costume.[54] Ewtoto symbolizes the spirit of Matsito, the original Bear clan ancestor to whom Maasaw gave stewardship of the Hopi land. Being buried as Ewtoto signaled the revocation of Maasaw's gift and the end of ceremonialism at Oraibi. Thus, Tawaquaptewa's act symbolized the end of precontact Hopi life and the beginning of an era in which a dominant society was to be confronted existentially. Tawaquaptewa also felt, however, that after an imminent famine had taken its course, the full ceremonial cycle might be revived, hence revealing his paradoxical understanding that the modern changes were only temporary within a larger framework of continuous cosmic cycles.[55]

Assimilation Pressures

After the split of Oraibi the federal government intensified its efforts to "convert" and "civilize" the Hopi people. Hopi children, like other Native Americans, were rounded up and sent to schools "to encourage them to become Christians and live like white men," according to the Hopi Fred Kabotie. The pressure exerted on Hopi children, often in the form of corporal punishment, was overwhelming, and several Hopis, including Kabotie, experienced a period of wishing they were white.[56]

Indeed, the first thirty years of the twentieth century saw an intensified effort by the federal government to assimilate all Native Americans.[57] The Hopi, of course, were no exception. In 1904, for example, a number of Hopi men were forced by the Indian agent Charles Burton to have their hair cut, an act that disregarded the ceremonial purpose of traditional hair styles.[58] Hopi men grew their hair long in the back as a symbol of the falling rain for which they prayed.[59] Given that Hopi prayers are always embodied within some material object, one can see the gravity of Burton's act. Furthermore, Hopi men liken their hair to the silken hairs that grow from ears of corn. Therefore, it was considered improper to cut hair during the growing season, for to do so was tantamount to a request that the corn stop growing.[60]

Not only Burton but also the school superintendents and federal agents Abraham Lawshe and Leo Crane, who served from 1910 to 1919, viewed the Hopi as somewhat less than human.[61] Crane, whose book *The Enchanted Desert* contains important information on the Hopi, wrote that "they begin as children to live on a moral plane little above their livestock."[62] Crane's successor, agent Robert Daniel, was no better. On June 10, 1921, he publicly deloused all Hopis in Hotevilla with sheep dip. Hopi men who attempted to stop this treatment, which included the public stripping and "bathing" of women, were brutally beaten, then arrested and jailed. Daniel became increasingly belligerent until he was finally released from duty in 1924. Daniel's successor, Edgar Miller, changed the name of the agency from Moqui (the old Spanish term for Hopi), to Hopi, a long overdue acceptance of the Hopi's self-identity. But the departure of Daniel hardly signaled better times for the Hopi.

In 1921 President Warren Harding appointed Albert Fall secretary of the interior. Fall's desire to exploit Native Americans unmercifully through his commissioner of Indian affairs, Charles Burke, aroused the anger of many American citizens who were sympathetic to the Native American plight. Fall immediately enacted a regulation prohibiting the Plains Indians from participating in the Sun Dance. He soon concluded that "all similar dances and so-called religious ceremonies, shall be considered 'Indian offences' " punishable by "incarceration in the agency prison for a period not exceeding thirty days."[63]

The Hopi soon learned of Fall's campaign to eliminate native religious rites through Indian Bureau officials who advised them that their religion would not be spared. Concern among the Hopi rose rapidly, and in 1922 the federal government asked several Hopi leaders to meet with bureau representatives in Winslow to discuss the matter. James Schultz was chosen to represent the government. A renowned expert on Indian affairs, Schultz listened attentively and sympathetically to the concerns of the Hopi leaders. As the discussion proceeded for some time, one Hopi elder jumped to his feet and exclaimed that he would rather be shot down while "doing his religion" than give it up. Schultz then told the Hopi that they should continue to practice their ceremonies and that many influential white people would back his decision. The Hopi stood firm and continued to observe their traditional ceremonial calendar. Although they received warnings from time to time from bureau officials, no substantial moves were ever made to interfere directly. In 1923 Fall was forced to resign.

A Turning Point

Public opinion has now swayed firmly to the side of Native American rights. In 1924, largely owing to the efforts of Indian Welfare League member Ida May Adams, Congress granted all Native Americans U.S. citizenship.[64] The general consensus of those concerned with Indian rights was that citizenship would give them freedom of religion under the Bill of Rights. Still, such freedom was more easily granted than lived. Fall's notoriety, however, and his subsequent imprisonment for taking bribes helped rally support behind the quest for Native American rights. This movement culminated in 1934 with passage of the Wheeler-Howard Act, better known as the Indian Reorganization Act, a turning point in Washington's official attitude toward Native Americans. The intention of the act was to allow Native Americans to govern their own affairs as much as possible within the structure of the U.S. Constitution. A Bureau of Indian Affairs was established, and John

Collier became its first superintendent. One of his first proposed programs was for each Indian tribe to form a tribal council to deal with the federal government in a way that the government could understand. Given the multiplicity of political structures of the Native American peoples, it becomes easier to sympathize with Collier's intention.[65]

In 1936 Collier requested that Oliver La Farge undertake the task of trying to convince the Hopi to form a council. With some reservations, he accepted the challenge. La Farge was aided by Superintendent Alexander Hutton in trying to convince the Hopi to accept Collier's plan. At first only Christian Hopis and those who worked for the Bureau of Indian Affairs were in favor of it, but they were enough to swing a final vote, given that those opposed simply abstained from voting.

The first Hopi Tribal Council meeting, held in 1937, was not very successful owing to opposition from traditionalists. Traditional Hopi political organization is centered on the *kikmongwi* (village chief) of each separate village. The Tribal Council, by contrast, is based on elected officials from each village, the number of representatives being determined by population. In other words, the Tribal Council is essentially based on a democratic form of government, not on clan relations. Moreover, its jurisdiction is tribalwide, whereas traditional Hopi government gave each village autonomy. Hopis resist any forced change that disrupts religious traditions; therefore opposition to the Tribal Council was inevitable. The Tribal Council stirred great controversy from its inception and was dissolved at one point, only to be reorganized in 1951. Today it still faces some opposition but clearly is functioning more smoothly and productively than it was initially, except perhaps on First Mesa.[66]

In fact, the so-called division of contemporary Hopis into "traditional" and "progressive" factions seems to have emerged from the positions taken with regard to the Tribal Council. Those who reject "reorganization" are labeled "traditionals," and those who accept it are termed "progressives." A closer examination of these terms reveals that they are essentially terms attributed to Hopis by whites.[67] That is to say, the terms mean little or nothing to most

Hopis. When asked whether they are traditionalist or progressive, Hopis usually answer, "I am a Hopi."[68] Indeed, attempts by anthropologist Shuichi Nagata to find Hopi terms for *traditional* and *progressive* proved futile.[69] He discovered that Upper ("progressive") Moencopi villagers were most frequently called *kansul* or *kansulhoyam* ("little council people"), while residents of Lower ("traditional") Moencopi were labeled *aiyave* ("nonconformists"). He also noted that these terms were used by both factions and that the English terms *progressive* and *traditional* were specifically avoided.

My own field research confirms Nagata's discovery. The Hopi I know avoid the traditional/progressive dichotomy and claim it has no usage except among a small group of primarily Hotevillans led by Thomas Banyacya. For the most part, the terms are stereotypical labels used by white Americans that do not correspond to native experience. Or, when they do, it is most often because the stereotypes are accepted by those who feel especially dominated. Just as some Native Americans accept the term *Indian*, which is clearly an invention of whites, some Hopis accept their division into progressive and traditional camps.[70] Still, Hopi factions show the impact of white society on Hopi identity, for each faction is defined with reference to the dominant government.

Five

Compartmentalization and Prophecy

Few Hopis are intrinsically fond of the Tribal Council, for its very existence presupposes a forced response to a dominant culture. The Hopi wish to follow their own path but cannot do so today without serious qualification. Indeed, Hopis still perceive the *kikmongwi* (village chief) as the spiritual leader of each village who is to lead his "children" by examples of humility, hard work, and good thoughts. Even today, when a village chief fails to follow the proper path the Hopi are quick to criticize him in terms of ancestral principles.[1]

Realizing the quandary they are in, the Hopi have devised a way of dealing with Washington while simultaneously preserving their traditions, or at least their underlying religious values. Emory Sekaquaptewa calls this process "compartmentalization"—a word derived from the work of Edward Spicer—and says it is the Hopi's way of keeping the two worlds separate.[2] Compartmentalization has at least two interrelated dimensions. First, it refers to the Hopi's ability to put in abeyance their traditional values while participating in another, dominant society. Such an imaginative process is perceived as necessary to preserve many traditional religious values. In other words, it is a means to an end. For example, the Hopi today may become involved in various nontraditional Western activities, such as formal education and litigation, precisely to preserve something traditional, such as sacred shrines or boundaries.[3] Helen Sekaquaptewa, in her autobiography, *Me and Mine,* related some advice her father gave to her sons when he was very old:

> You of the younger generation, stand for what is right. Go to school and be diligent, don't play around, but learn the white man's language and his ways so you can come back and help your people and fight the *pahana* in his own way. Who knows? It might be one of you to save our land. The Navajos are living on our land and keep encroaching farther. We must get them off. It is our land and we must have it. It will be a ticklish job to get our land away from the Navajos. It will take men of courage and patience and integrity and other virtues to stand up to them. Get an order from the government and do it in a legal way and don't give up.[4]

These remarks are echoed today by many Hopis who are involved in legal and political professions in order to keep their sacred lands. Other Hopis may take up wage-earning jobs to raise the money necessary to educate their children so that they may be self-sufficient and become actively involved in the quest for the recovery of lands now occupied by Navajos. To keep their current lands and to recover parts now occupied by others, the Hopi must fight within the judicial and legislative framework of the dominant society, and that requires money. Again, though, the acquisition of money is not an end in itself for most Hopis; it is part of a program whereby they communicate with Washington in order to preserve their heritage.

Abbot Sekaquaptewa once related a story that demonstrates this first dimension of compartmentalization. One day he encountered one of his nieces, a Bureau of Indian Affairs schoolteacher involved in helping the Hopi attain self-determination through formal education. She explained that she was out of work that day owing to a lack of operating funds. "Oh well," she said, "it gives me a chance to stay home all day and grind corn."[5] Her remarks exemplify compartmentalization as a process in which the Hopi put aside traditional values at times so that they may survive in a dominant society while, nonetheless, preserving their sacred ancestry.

A second, yet conjoined, aspect of compartmentalization is the

Hopi attempt to embody traditional values within a nontraditional modality. Here the goal is not to place traditional values in abeyance but rather to embody them through the employment of a nontraditional mode. Emory Sekaquaptewa has written, for example, that the Hopi must no longer dwell on the fact that many traditional practices have no place in dealing with the Bureau of Indian Affairs. Rather, the Hopi should seek a way to implement the traditional values underlying those traditions within the Hopi Constitution.[6] Of course, that is a difficult task, especially since the Hopi Constitution was written largely by the Bureau of Indian Affairs,[7] one of the reasons many Hopi think a new constitution is warranted. Even so, the Hopi Constitution, by giving each village political autonomy, including respect for the village chief, attempts in writing to preserve the religiopolitical essence of the Hopi's traditional government. Such attempts permeate the Hopi Constitution and reveal one way in which the Hopi seek to come to terms with their conqueror in an authentic, religious manner. The Hopi are fully aware that they cannot simply return to their past way of life,[8] but they also refuse to acquiesce to the "civilizing" structures of the United States.

Thomas Banyacya's group, which refuses to accept, willingly, any imposed twentieth-century change, feels that a return to the past is impossible. They view the disintegration of Hopi religiosity as one sign of the prophesied end of the world, which they think is almost here.[9] Nonetheless, some traditionals, including Banyacya, are still willing to fight for the return of all lost traditional lands.[10] Criticizing the decision of Abbot Sekaquaptewa's administration to accept five million dollars as compensation for lost lands, Banyacya argues that acceptance of the proposed land-claim settlement could extinguish any hopes of ever recovering the land in question. It is difficult to gauge the intentions of the council when it proposed accepting the settlement, but it seems unlikely that the council simply acquiesced to the dominant society. As Jake Page has noted, the five-million-dollar settlement means only that the Hopi agreed to seek no more money from the federal government for lost land.[11] More important, the council argued without compromise that traditional land boundaries should be recognized by the federal government. That the federal government refused to accept the claim is another matter. At least with a settlement the Hopi would gain capital needed to continue other important struggles for self-determination, which they might win. It indeed seems unlikely that the federal government is going to displace thousands and thousands of Navajos who inhabit lands traditionally held by the Hopi,[12] and such thinking motivated Abbot Sekaquaptewa's administration to accept the proposed settlement. Besides, settlement or not, the Hopi feel that their land may one day be returned to them by their creator.

Another congressional move related to the Indian Reorganization Act that affected the Hopi is the Stock Reduction Program of 1944.[13] Based on the fact that increased sheepherding was resulting in overgrazed lands, this act brought a shift from sheep to cattle and the reduction of the number of horses on the reservation. Cattle require much less care than do sheep and do not graze so close to the ground, thus preserving more grass. By shifting to cattle, the Hopi were able to herd for profit, and thus, as Edward Kennard wrote, the Stock Reduction Program witnessed a change "from a subsistence economy supplemented by cash and trade goods to a cash economy supplemented by the persistence of traditional subsistence activities."[14] Furthermore, the reduced number of horses, combined with an increase in wage earnings, led to an increased use of motor vehicles.

The use of motor vehicles was enhanced when many roads were paved in the 1950s and 1960s. These roads, which linked the Hopi with various surrounding towns, such as Winslow and Flagstaff, made the Hopi more accessible than before.[15] Soon supermarkets in those cities began to replace the reservation trading posts, and several Hopis began to heat and cook with gas rather than wood.[16] Job opportunities increased among Hopis, and a number of specialized skills developed, affecting various traditions, such as house building.

Today many Hopi houses are no longer constructed of rock quarried from a mesa and mortar dug from the valley floor. Instead, construction materials are purchased from building-supply companies and are used by Hopi carpenters to build nontraditional houses, though many look a bit like the old pueblos. It is important to note, however, that it is often cheaper for Hopis to build today with cinder block than with native sandstone, and the Hopi people are financially poor.[17] Given the time, knowledge, and resources needed to construct a house from handcut stone and the necessity of wage earning to maintain their autonomy, it is understandable that many Hopis choose to build cheaply.[18]

Similarly, it also seems as though use of running water is now cheaper than hauling water in from wells on trucks (though it is not cheaper than hauling water by hand—a very time-consuming method).[19] It is also understandable that ceremonies are now held for the most part on weekends, since most adults earn wages during the week. Hopi ceremonies require much food sharing and gift giving, and therefore, on a positive note, wage earning has brought an increase in the number of kachina dances held from May until the Home Dance ceremony in July. Before World War II (and the Stock Reduction Program), each Hopi village was usually able to sponsor only one kachina dance before Home Dance. Since then one or more villages generally sponsor a dance each week during the outside dance season.[20]

At the same time, one must ask whether Hopi ceremonies are still performed for religious reasons. Kennard talked with an old Hopi in 1965 who said that many Hopis dance no longer for rain but for showing how well they are doing.[21] Furthermore, Abbot Sekaquaptewa has reminded us that widespread participation in kachina ceremonies is no indication of the strength of Hopi religion, since many priesthoods are weak.[22] I discussed earlier the infrequency or lack of Wuwtsim initiations among the Hopi that, coupled with improper perceptions of Kachina clan ceremonies, indicates serious problems. One elder from Third Mesa distinguishes two aspects of ceremonies, cultural and religious. He goes on to say that on Third Mesa only the cultural element survives. After all, most ceremonial leaders on Third Mesa do not reside in Hotevilla; most went from Oraibi to Bacavi, where no major rites are held today.[23]

Perhaps such changes parallel the growth in the number of Hopis who no longer farm seriously. The Hopi ceremonial cycle is inseparably linked with traditional Hopi subsistence activities, such as farming. One old Hopi man confirmed the relationship of farming and ritual when he asked, "How can you pray for rain if you don't have a field?"[24] It seems to me that the broader question asked by the old Hopi is this: how can one pray for rain if one is not existentially engaged with the world, whether through hunting, gathering, herding, building, or farming? The number of acres farmed has dropped considerably.[25] I do not wish to imply that the meaning of Hopi prayer is reducible to a concern for crops and other material blessings any more than I wish to say that Hopi subsistence modes are reducible to a desire to experience ultimacy and transcendence. I cannot predict what will become of Hopi religious experience when and if more changes in the material cultures are embodied, for I am a historian, not a prophet. Only time will tell whether an increased emphasis on nontraditional subsistence activities will significantly alter Hopi religiosity. If such directed (forced) changes are perceived as compartmentalized or mythicized/prophesied, however, then their influence on constitutive religious structures will be minimal. For example, take the issue of language loss among the Hopi.[26] That young Hopis speak Hopi less and less is a pervasive problem at Hopi today. Learning the Hopi language is bound up with the entire traditional philosophy of childrearing and education. Thus Hopis have resisted teaching the Hopi language in Bureau of Indian Affairs schools up to now. Some still oppose it and feel that if it cannot be taught as part of the Hopi way, it should die, as prophesied. Others, including a ceremonial chief from Second Mesa, argue that Hopi should be taught in school to prevent its dying, realizing that such a change in contexts is forced by the dominant society.[27]

Land Problems

Emory Sekaquaptewa has written that no matter what response to modernity the Hopis make, whether progressive or traditional, the chief issue is land.[28] And land problems continue to mount. Ironically, with regard to land disputes, the Hopi's main antagonists are another Native American group, the Navajo, although Washington oversees the politics of both tribes. The Hopi have had conflicts with Navajos over land boundaries ever since Navajos migrated into the Hopi region from the northwest at some unknown date. Navajos have consistently encroached on Hopi lands and have been given some traditional Hopi lands by the federal government.

The Hopi are thus in a precarious three-way relationship with Navajos and whites. Both the Navajo and the whites have attempted to conquer the Hopi, and the Hopi have somehow managed to resist. Sometimes it seems that the Hopi do not know who is a greater threat, the Americans or the Navajo. Both have caused the Hopi much grief and suffering. Don Talayesva's remarks about this three-way tension summarize the opinions of many Hopis: "We might be better off if the Whites had never come to Oraibi, but that was impossible, for the world is full of them, while in numbers we Hopi are as nothing. Now we have learned to get along with them, in a manner, and we would probably live much worse if they left us to ourselves and to the Navajos."[29] Talayesva may well be correct, for the Navajo number about 180,000 to only 11,000 Hopis. Therefore, in one sense the Hopi are fortunate to have the United States as an arbiter of the land disputes between themselves and the Navajo.

At the same time Washington is part and parcel of the Hopi-Navajo dispute, for the Hopi reservation proposed in 1882 gave some traditional Hopi lands to the Navajo. Then in 1962 the federal government gave additional lands to the Navajo by dividing 1.8 million acres of the 1882 reservation between the two tribes.[30] Finally, in 1977 the so-called joint use area was divided equally between Hopis and Navajos, the western and southern sectors going to the Hopi, the eastern and northern sectors to the Navajo.[31] Since then the government has spent millions of dollars in an attempt to relocate about 10,000 Navajos who settled Hopi lands.[32] The involvement of the federal government in the Hopi-Navajo problem, at a fundamental level, reflects the government's power over both peoples. While it is true that the Hopi and Navajo experienced serious tensions and problems before the arrival of the white Americans, they no doubt dealt with those issues differently than they did after their encounters with white people. Both groups recognize the superior political power of the government, and they realize that the government could at any time determine their destinies in the short term to a large extent. Even if both groups were to express themselves as they wished, it would be only because the white Americans granted them the right to self-expression. Thus it may be fair to say that the Hopi benefit politically from federal government assistance in dealing with the stronger Navajo, but the fact that such beneficial power resides within a dominant, outside culture reveals at a basic structural level the emergence of a situation very different from the one that existed before contact. Then, the Hopi and Navajo would have worked their problems out in their own way, rather than coming to terms with each other through the mediation of a dominant third party.

Today the disputes over land between Hopis and Navajos and Hopis and Americans continue to be settled in federal court. The Hopi tribe recently tried to prevent further commercial development of the San Francisco Peaks outside Flagstaff. Arguing that the expansion of the Snow Bowl ski resort would profane a kachina shrine vital to their religion, the Hopi tried unsuccessfully to block construction legally via the First Amendment principle of religious freedom.[33] The fight over Snow Bowl is a good example of compartmentalization in which the Hopi participate in a nontraditional activity in order to preserve what matters to them most— their sacred land. To be a Hopi today requires certain actions that were not necessary even a century ago. The purpose of many of those activities, however, is to come to terms with a dominant society so that the Hopi can continue to live many of their religious values.

Still, the Hopi remain disappointed at the failure of the United States government to act upon many legal decisions rendered in the courts that favor the Hopi over the Navajo. The Hopi often lament that though they have historically cooperated well with Washington, they have rarely received justice.[34] When Hopis win in court, they struggle to have the decisions executed. Citing numerous instances in which Navajos have received preferential treatment by Washington in Hopi-Navajo disputes, the Hopi offer two reasons. First, the Hopi argue that the numerically stronger Navajos have greater political power and influence over the federal government than do the Hopi. According to the Hopi, the Navajo represent more potential votes and more lobbying power and, therefore, are favored by most politicians.[35] The courts, however, are bound by laws and justice and have awarded the Hopi a number of decisions over the Navajo. A second reason Hopis cite for suffering injustice is related to prophecy. Hopi elders have prophesied a time when the Hopi will suffer exploitation and injustice at the hands of a dominant people. Understanding that prophecy as fulfilled, the Hopi resign themselves to the current political situation, for the prophecy also holds that a way to endure will be provided. In the meantime, it is hoped by all concerned that the Navajo-Hopi conflict can be worked out harmoniously.

When Ivan Sidney and Peter Zah, old acquaintances, were elected tribal chairmen of the Hopi and Navajo respectively, there was optimism regarding possible solutions to their ancient problems. Both parties realized the political advantage of cooperating with each other whenever dealing with Washington.[36] However, both men agree that any long-term solution to the land disputes will require the cooperation of all concerned, and no such harmony was realized during Zah's term.

Indeed, in 1983 and 1984 several Hopi men were harassed by Navajos while gathering eagles for an upcoming Home Dance.[37] Navajo policemen on the scene claimed to be ignorant of a government-issued permit that allows Hopis to hunt eagles on Hopi traditional lands given to the Navajo in 1882. In 1988 Navajo policemen issued criminal citations to four Hopis who were gathering eagles in traditional gathering areas near Gap, Arizona. The charges were later dropped, but as the vice chairman of the Hopi tribe Vernon Masayesva noted at a hearing before the United States Commission on Civil Rights, the Hopi were in effect prevented from gathering eagles for religious purposes in 1988. Thus not only do Navajos continue to build on Hopi lands, but they also continue to harass Hopis who have legitimate permits to enter Navajo lands once held by the Hopi.

Coal Mining

The Hopi face another problem that concerns the contract they signed with Peabody Coal Company in 1969.[39] That agreement allows coal to be strip mined on Black Mesa to the northwest of the villages. Some Hopis have opposed the contract since its inception because of their perception of strip mining as an irreverent use of their sacred land. The problems surrounding this controversial issue are complex and embody a religious dimension that makes them of ultimate concern to Hopis.

The Hopi, however, mined coal prehistorically, before the coming of the Spanish, and thus it cannot be argued rightly that coal mining in and of itself is nontraditional or irreligious. John Hack wrote an important paper in which he demonstrated that the Hopi mined coal from the thirteenth to the seventeenth centuries.[40] The Hopi may have been the only Native Americans to mine coal prehistorically, and they may have been the first people in the world to do so. Coal was primarily strip mined, though at least one area was mined by underground methods. Lacking sufficient data, Hack could only speculate as to why the Hopi abandoned coal mining in the seventeenth century. Perhaps by the time of Spanish arrival, easily available deposits were exhausted. Such seems to have been the case at Awatobi, for example. Perhaps the Spanish introduction of the burro and the iron ax made wood gathering more feasible, and that, combined with the exhaustion of surface coal deposits, led to a revival of wood use. Or, as one Hopi related, the noxious fumes produced by coal burning may have led to its cessation, except for firing pottery outside.[41] As for why wood was ever abandoned for coal, Hack suggested that the pinyon-juniper forests were pushed far away from the villages in the thirteenth century by timbering or climatic change or both. Or it may be that once discovered, coal proved to be easier to obtain than wood, which had to be cut with crude stone tools. At any rate, it seems obvious that for four centuries the Hopi spent considerable time and energy mining and using coal.

Still, there are Hopis who oppose coal mining and feel that

Peabody Coal is exploiting the earth mother. Such feelings are not exclusive to the Hopi. For example, Mircea Eliade wrote that all over the world miners practice purification rituals because they are about to enter a sacred zone that is taboo.[42] Furthermore, miners are entering the womb of the earth to acquire something for rapid consumption that took thousands of years to gestate. That in itself makes mining a rather haughty act, for minerals are depleted much faster than the sacred replenishes them.

The available archaeological and ethnological evidence seems to indicate that when the Hopi mined prehistorically, the mining paralleled no major changes in their life-style. Apparently no special priesthood emerged with regard to mining, although perhaps miners were warriors who came from those clans that claim Maasaw as ancestor. It is known that when the Hopi undertook pilgrimages to gather salt in the Grand Canyon, they also dug for a special yellowish clay that is found under the ground near the original sacred center. To dig this clay is to enter the underworld realm of the spiritual and must be done properly according to the teaching of the ancestors. Furthermore, the War chief must accompany the expedition, for entering the land of the dead is dangerous and requires the presence of one who is related to the god of death, Maasaw.[43] Talayesva noted in his autobiography that before the salt and clay pilgrimage, breath feathers were constructed "for the Kachinas, Clouds, and the dead who live in the underworld" and who "own" its contents. As the youngest member of the expedition, Talayesva was required to dig for the sacred clay and was instructed to keep his "mind and heart full of good wishes" to ward off death. The entire operation was perceived passively or receptively, the Hopi acquiring that which the sacred wished to give. Therefore, after a couple of attempts, Talayesva dug no more, for his father "remarked that the spirits had decided we had enough for this time."[44] The religious understanding of mining by Hopis is borne out by a mining event that occurred on Second Mesa. Ernest Beaglehole related that Mishongnovi men stopped mining coal from the north side of Second Mesa after a man was killed there by falling rocks while mining. The Mishongnovi villagers interpreted the man's death as a sign from the gods that no more coal was to be taken from there.[45] It appears that the Hopi may mine coal if proper ritual precautions are taken unless the gods signal otherwise.

Contemporary Hopis who support coal mining on Black Mesa note that there are no prophecies forbidding coal mining there. Abbot Sekaquaptewa has said that "the important thing is not that we mine, but how we do it. Before the first shovel was turned at Black Mesa, the land was barren, overgrazed, and without growth. Now grasses are coming up in the places where the shovels worked. Those grasses feed not only our livestock but all the animals of the ecological chain."[46] Those Hopis who continue to oppose the strip mining of Black Mesa are quick to point out that air pollution stemming from nearby generating plants has made accurate observances of sunrise for ceremonial purposes difficult at times. Given the importance of the Hopi ceremonial calendar for maintaining life, one can see the life-threatening problem raised by the commercial burning of coal. Indeed, Fred Kabotie, who originally supported the Black Mesa project because it would generate revenues for the tribe, wrote in his autobiography that he questioned whether the Hopi did the right thing in signing the contract with Peabody.[47] Some Hopis oppose the mining of Black Mesa because eagle nesting sites in that area are being disturbed and many eagles have abandoned them.[48] According to Hopi tradition, eagles are spiritual beings used to construct breath feathers and prayer sticks; thus the loss of eagles has religious consequences. Other Hopi opponents of the Black Mesa project cite the waste of precious groundwater resulting from the slurrying of coal dust from the mine to generating plants. In slurrying, coal dust is mixed with equal parts of water and pumped through pipes. The process is cheaper than hauling coal by trucks because groundwater is free of charge. For the Hopi, however, groundwater contains the "spiritual substance" upon which all life forms depend, and therefore a number of Hopis object to the removal of millions of gallons of water a day for the purpose of saving Peabody Coal Company money.

Richard Clemmer has offered some valuable insights into why some Hopis accepted Peabody's offer.[49] Clemmer argued that the

Hopi were covertly forced into accepting a contract proposal from Peabody by the federal government. Once large coal deposits were discovered, the Hopi were no longer able to seclude themselves in the desert, and they became conscious of the tenuousness of their land rights. Therefore, when government authorities began exerting pressure on the Hopi to lease their coal reserves to Peabody in order to generate power for cities in the region, the Hopi leaders were wise enough to cooperate. Clemmer noted that not only were the Hopi forced to allow their land to be mined but were also offered royalties well below market price, again demonstrating their subjection to dominance.

I would add that the exploitive character of the Hopi-Peabody contract is further revealed by the fact that Peabody does not use trucks to transport the mined coal to its generating plants. Trucking would cost more but would help its relationship with the Hopi (and the earth) by saving trillions of gallons of ground water.[50] Because they have not done so and because the Hopi are losing valuable resources for very little profit, the Hopi decided in 1982 to enact a severance fee on all coal mined from Black Mesa to ensure that future generations of Hopis would one day reap some benefit.[51] But the severance fee proposed was vetoed by the assistant secretary of the interior for Indian affairs, again raising the problem of self-determination in the minds of the Hopi.[52] The Hopi then worked out another plan for the fee, and again it was vetoed by Washington.[53]

Self-Determination

President Richard Nixon first introduced the idea of Native American self-determination, an idea that the Reagan administration also favored.[54] While appearing to be positive at first glance, policies allowing Native Americans to set their own course are viewed cautiously by Native Americans, who fear further exploitation. The Hopi feel that Washington's self-determination policy may be a cover to allow the federal government to withdraw financial and political support of peoples such as the Hopi. The Hopi feel that the federal government is an integral part of the problems that they now face, and thus they see an abrupt pullout by Washington as still another form of dominance. For example, the federal government was directly involved in the assignment of lands to the Hopi and the Navajo in the nineteenth century. Thus they were responsible in part for the loss of some traditional lands by Hopis that were given to the Navajo. Given that, the Hopi feel that it is only fair that Washington serve as mediator in the Hopi-Navajo land disputes. Washington's withdrawal from that problem would be perceived by the Hopi as an act of domination by passivity, for then the Hopi would be pitted directly against the numerically and politically stronger Navajos and white Americans.

It seems that most Hopis desire complete self-sufficiency but realize that such a state of freedom is not feasible at this time. Accordingly, they view the federal government ambivalently, wanting it to protect their legal rights yet hoping to be treated as a free people. Perhaps Abbot Sekaquaptewa said it best: "Until we arrive at the point of true independence and self-sufficiency, we need to impress on the federal government the importance of honoring its legal obligations, while at the same time also honoring the principle of dealing with the Indian tribes as sovereign entities."[55]

Ironically, it was the fear of government aid withdrawal that led Hopi Tribal Chairman Ivan Sidney to oppose lobbying by Hopis to enact the coal severance fee ordinance. Though most Hopis may have resented Sidney's refusal to cooperate with the Tribal Council's directive, Sidney felt that to do so would be dangerous. While recognizing the need for Hopi self-determination, Sidney understood the need for gradual implementation of such a program. Because of that, he opposed the ordinance on the basis that its passage might evoke the withdrawal of federal support programs, forcing the Hopi "into the mainstream."[56]

But there is still another, more basic problem facing the Hopi in their quest for self-determination. How can the Hopi ever achieve true self-determination when the power to follow the Hopi way resides in the political policies of the dominant society? Put another way, can the Hopi ever be free within a larger society that has the power to grant and remove independence? Even if the Hopi become economically self-sufficient, it will only be because they choose and are allowed to participate fully in an economic system that is not commensurate with their deepest wishes.

Yet the Hopi simultaneously feel that their subjection to a dominant society was prophesied by elders in the long ago. One prophecy states that the Hopi will wake up one day in the midst of whites. Under those circumstances it will be necessary for the Hopi to learn the whites' language and thoughts so that the Hopi will not be confused. If the Hopi remain true to their life plan, however, the whites will follow the Hopi way of life after a purification day.[57] Thus, while the Hopi recognize the irreducible power that the whites exert over them today, they also understand that it may not last forever. In that sense, the Hopi continue to be oriented by traditional religious values passed down by their ancestors.

Other Issues

In the meantime, changes continue to take place among the Hopi. Shongopavi is currently the only village that conducts almost all major ceremonies in long form, but even there parts of the Butterfly Dance had to be taught in English for the first time in 1981. Several younger female dancers apparently were not fluent enough in their native tongue to understand the dance instructions and thus received their lessons in English.[58] The village of Hotevilla conducts some major ceremonies, but because of losses in key priesthood positions resulting from the Oraibi split, many rites are done in abbreviated form.[59] Still, Hotevilla is perceived as the most conservative and traditional of all villages (at least by Hotevillans), in part because it has not accepted electricity and running water. Hotevillans have, furthermore, best preserved the use of their native language, but even there English is spoken more and more by the young.[60]

Shongopavi has retained most of the Hopi ceremonial calendar but now has well water and electricity available, even though many elders resisted their introduction. In his autobiography, Fred Kabotie related his hard struggle to convince the villagers of Shongopavi to dig a well to ease water acquisition efforts.[61] According to him, it is important for Hopis to preserve their religion and culture, but in so doing they need not reject all modern influence. Kabotie thinks that the important thing is that young Hopi grow up healthy and participate in the traditional ceremonial cycle. To him, there seems to be no real problem between participating in the ritual calendar and receiving well water, electricity, and sanitation. On the other hand, those who opposed the Shongopavi well project did so because they felt that it would make life too easy, thereby encouraging the growth of bad thoughts and bad hearts.[62] Indeed, for a long time many Shongopavi residents continued to bring water up the mesa from springs below, although an elderly woman told me that some of those same people can be seen drawing water from the well late at night.

The Shongopavi state of affairs raises some interesting problems that I think are applicable to all Hopis today. It seems to me that Hopi religiosity and authenticity may not necessarily be necessarily undermined by the introduction of running water. In and of itself, the adoption of running water is not the question. Rather, the question for the Hopi is whether the adoption of plumbing will adversely affect traditional Hopi values, such as hard work, humility, and maintaining a good heart. Indeed, such is the case for even the Hopi traditionalists, who say that they will accept modern technology when it does not "violate their religious traditions and religious lands."[63] Those values are integral components in Hopi prayer acts that are essential for preserving life in the desert environment. Hopis such as Fred Kabotie apparently feel that certain modern conveniences do not necessarily make life easy given the other problems that the Hopi must address, and therefore they are willing to adopt some external forms. Along similar lines, Abbot Sekaquaptewa has written that the Hopi can probably be forgiven for taking up wage-earning jobs and certain modern conveniences, for the Hopi must maintain a standard of living comparable to that of the dominant society in which they live.[64] For some, running water may simply make life easier; but when one has a job that takes one off the reservation five or six days a week for eight to twelve hours a day, it becomes a virtual necessity. Thus a number of Hopi compartmentalize their use of plumbing as a necessity forced upon them by a dominant society.

The total picture includes another plane of understanding as well. One widespread Hopi prophecy found especially today on Third Mesa holds that whites will offer the Hopi both good and bad and that the Hopi must be careful to choose only the good. For some Hopis running water may be perceived as a helpful and appropriate acquisition from the Americans. And in either case, the adoption of running water is understood to have been prophesied from the beginning. The prophetic interpretation of borrowings from white people seems to hinge not so much on the phenomenon in question as on its eventual impact on the religious quality of Hopi life. If the use of running water is perceived to undermine traditional religious values, it is either avoided or compartmentalized; if it is seen as helpful to the Hopi, it is accepted openly. The Hopi differ from clan to clan, village to village, and mesa to mesa as to what they find appropriate to borrow from whites, but all make their decision based on their understanding of the religious principles of the Hopi way.

That is generally true even for those few Hopis who enter mainstream American society. Many Hopis who have left the reservation for work in various cities often lament the loss of life at "home." Though they seem thoroughly Westernized at first glance, they nonetheless retain at least memories of their spiritual upbringing if not the desire to return one day to live. One Hopi, Dennis Nukema, who left Moencopi to become an architect in Phoenix, claimed once to be "about as urban a Hopi as you will meet." Yet even he wanted to go home someday to live and said he would do so if he could find a job comparable to the one he had. He admitted to being a product of the Western world, and yet his break with Hopi was hardly final. He still found religious solace there periodically. As he noted, "I have a yearning every once in a while to go up there, but I have become a product of this world here. . . . I go back for relief from all the turmoil. When I am 'home,' I am so comfortable. One cannot be in a more appropriate environment. It's very spiritual."[65]

Fred Kabotie was very influential in promoting the commercial selling of Hopi arts and crafts after World War II and in building the Hopi Cultural Center.[66] Today there is serious talk about expanding the Hopi Museum to help preserve Hopi religion and culture and to regulate research carried out on the reservation.[67] Kabotie was one of the first Hopis to use commercial painting as a means of interpreting Hopi traditions to non-Hopi. His son, Michael, and several others formed a guild in 1973 called Artist Hopid that also seeks to interpret Hopi traditions by and through nontraditional art forms.[68] Such a process seems to embody traditional values in a nontraditional way. I have found the commercial art work of most Hopis to be striking and deeply meaningful. I remember, for example, in 1981 seeing a self-portrait by Michael Kabotie in which part of his face was a mesa edge. The portrait seemed to say that the Hopi's sacred land continues to define the identity and essence of the Hopi people.

This same message is also found in two recently acquired Hopi art forms, photography and poetry. In 1983 several Hopis put together a small collection of their photographs and poems. The result was *Hopi Photographers/Hopi Images*, a book that attempts to use nontraditional modes of communication to present the essence of the Hopi way to non-Hopis. Again, though, the process of compartmentalization raises an interesting and serious problem: can the Hopi preserve the authenticity of their orientation by attempting to embody traditional spiritual values within Western formats? The problem is acknowledged among the Hopi and is a constitutive feature of the ambivalence which Hopis today experience.

Victor Masayesva related this sense of ambivalence in his introduction to *Hopi Photographers/Hopi Images*. While photographing a Hopi elder, he was called a Kwikwilyaqa by his subject.[69] After reflecting on the matter Masayesva concluded that the old Hopi man intended two messages in his remark. Kwikwilyaqa is a kachina whose face is black and white with three protruding tubes for eyes and mouth. Masayesva noted that his camera resembled Kwikwilyaqa's face and thus concluded that he did indeed look like a Kwikwilyaqa to the old Hopi man. But Kwikwilyaqa also mocks or copies whatever he sees.[70] He is generally seen dressed as a white man, indicating that he has copied the manners of another people. Masayesva suggested that perhaps one meaning of the old man's remark was that the very act of photography, regardless of how it is done, is borrowed from the West and represents a loss of identity for the Hopi who use it seriously. While his intentions might be honorable and authentic, Masayesva wondered whether authentic Hopi values could be retained within such a non-Hopi modality.

Again, then, it seems to me that the Hopi today accept or reject a Western innovation according to whether or not that novelty will hurt Hopi religiosity. Such an understanding helps illuminate why there is so much variation between villages with regard to Western influence. I mentioned earlier that Shongopavi is the most traditional village ceremonially but has electricity and running water. By contrast, Hotevillans today perform fewer ceremonies, yet they, up to now, still refuse to install plumbing and electricity. Oraibi residents perform few rites, although they feel the ceremonial calendar may be resuscitated eventually (indeed, a kachina ceremony was conducted there in 1984[71]). But they feel that the problems raised by adopting electricity and plumbing are overwhelming and thus refuse them.[72] Years ago, Don Talayesva indicated that he might like to have running water but not a radio or electricity.[73] Furthermore, on Third Mesa the decline of ceremonialism is viewed paradoxically as preserving the integrity of Hopi religion since it was decided in Oraibi that the rites should end. Once the ceremonial calendar became corrupt and impure (as prophesied), Oraibis felt that it was better to discontinue the cycle than to perform the ceremonies in profane form. Few ceremonies are performed at Bacavi; yet all households and families there continue to practice Hopi dry farming at some level.[74] The Bacavis, like the Oraibis, discontinued the ceremonial cycle because of concern for traditional Hopi religious values. But they remain deeply spiritual as evidenced by their widespread participation in Hopi farming activities.

Walpi, while holding many ceremonies today, no longer has the main kiva society initiations.[75] Yet until 1983 the village of Walpi had no access to running water or electricity, and all its houses were built traditionally with sandstone.[76] The Walpians maintained traditional architectural forms through federal assistance, however, and most residents also owned more modern houses with utilities below in Polacca.

Thus there are several Hopi approaches to the problems of modernity. But in each case it is important to remember that Hopis base decisions on their perception of the consequences for traditional religious patterns. The issue is not whether the Hopi adopt certain aspects of the Western world but how those borrowings will affect their traditional religious values. In the meantime, problems mount.

One problem concerns the theft of sacred objects. The problem of white pot hunters is well known; many Hopi ancestral sites fall prey to greedy whites who sell priceless cultural artifacts in the criminal underground.[77] Even more tragic has been the loss of essential ritual objects on First and Second Mesas owing to theft by Hopis who attempt to sell these items to white collectors.[78] Most of these Hopis seem to be young men who are experiencing an identity crisis and feel little link with Hopi traditional values. Abbot Sekaquaptewa noted that such sacred items play an important part in initiating Hopi children into vital ceremonial societies and cannot be replaced immediately. Thus important ceremonial knowledge necessary for securing the blessing of life is being lost to younger Hopis. Indeed, the village of Shongopavi has not held Wuwtsim priesthood initiations since the early 1980s, raising the question of whether its ceremonial cycle will continue.

Still another problem confronting the Hopi is the improper possession and public display of sacred objects in various museums across the United States. Jake Page has written about Hopi attitudes toward the loss of ritual objects that end up in museum display cases.[79] Emory Sekaquaptewa noted that the handling of certain items by scholars profanes their purity.[80] While understanding the value of preserving various artifacts in museums, he is critical of collections that contribute to the demise of a living religious tradition.

A structurally similar problem confronting the Hopi is the imitation of their sacred dances by a white group called Smoki.[81]

Although members of the group claim they do not imitate fully any Native American rite, it is obvious to Hopis that the Smoki rites are based on Hopi ceremonies, such as the Snake Dance and various kachina dances. Hopi elders call the Smoki ceremonies sacrilege and have confronted the Smoki leaders several times about the improper performance of Hopi-inspired rituals. The Smokis claim they do no harm, although how they could know that is hardly made clear. Again the Hopi are confronted with whites who, in the name of preservation, are in fact eroding the sacredness of the Hopi way of life.

The Hopi are also confronted today with the problem of legally defining a Hopi tribal member.[82] Traditionally, the Hopi knew implicitly who they were, their identity being secured through birth, kinship patterns, and various initiation ceremonies. Other persons were from time to time adopted into the tribe or were allowed to live with the tribe through general consensus. Indeed, Hopi oral traditions hold that the Hopi are an amalgamation of various clans, many of which claim to have been at one time Apache, Ute, or Shoshoni.[83] Of course, once they migrated to Hopi and settled there, they embodied the Hopi way. Today the Hopi Constitution includes in writing the definition of a Hopi as well as procedures for adoption into the tribe. That is a difficult task. Again, the Hopi are attempting to embody traditional values within a Western framework.

Yet how can that be done when the meaning of a religious value is inseparable from its mode of manifestation?[84] That is to say, if Hopi membership was traditionally determined by largely unspoken, embodied perceptions, how can membership qualifications be put in writing? The Hopi have nevertheless sought a solution to this problem by submitting various proposed amendments to the Hopi Constitution concerning qualifications for tribal membership.[85] The proposals include a complex blood quantum formula that will be difficult to implement. Also proposed is an amendment that would abolish adoptions of non-Hopis into the tribe. The question of tribal membership is made difficult by the written word, but perhaps it is fair to say that the problem exists only in relation to its solution, that is to say, the solution helps define the problem. And yet the solution to the question of Hopi tribal membership is likely to undergo further changes in time, again manifesting the problem.

Many changes experienced by late twentieth-century Hopis are clearly forced upon them by white Americans, but some are not so clearly related to white dominance. For example, some Hopis lament the loss of ceremonial priesthoods and blame whites.[86] But Albert Yava for one says that in the end the Hopi can only blame themselves for the deterioration of their traditions. At the same time, Yava admits that maintaining traditional ways of life is virtually impossible in the face of a dominant culture that demands a certain amount of participation.[87] In fact, Yava, a fully initiated Hopi-Tewa, moved away from Hopi to the Colorado River Indian Reservation, which houses several tribes. He argues that the Hopi will one day assimilate completely into the mainstream society because it is necessary that they do so in order to survive. For Yava, the struggle for the preservation of the traditional values is secondary to life itself, and he feels that the Hopi must acquiesce to the dominant society in order to be.

Still, it is clear that most Hopis are critical of the way in which they have loosened their hold on ancient Hopi values. As early as 1942, Talayesva described the rapid loss of traditions as the Hopi began to adapt the whites' way of life. While Talayesva was witnessing a Spinach kachina *(Isöökatsina)* ceremony, his eyes filled with tears as he realized the disintegration of the Hopi way:

> We are spoiled by the white man's fancy foods and foolish clothes. Now the Hopi turns up his nose at the old-fashioned foods, and the day will come when no woman will dress in a decent Hopi way. I realized that the good old days are gone and that it is too late to bring them back. As the Katcinas danced, my mind was filled with these thoughts and I was so upset the tears ran down my face. It was clear that we could never be good Hopis again with our religion neglected and our ceremonies dying out. It is no wonder that we are weakened by disease and that death comes early—we are no longer Hopi, but kahopi [not Hopi].[88]

It is instructive to note that Talayesva sees the loss of Hopi religiosity as the most crucial and life-threatening problem faced by the Hopi today. Indeed, the same message is often communicated by various Hopis who are wrestling with the problems of modernity. For example, Alph Secakuku has written that

> whether we are willing to accept it or not, much of our belief, cultural practices and teachings have been lost. Often times we blame this great loss on the dominant cultures. Very seldom do we carefully perform self analysis and admit that we are at fault. . . . Whether we want to admit it or not, we are practicing our way of life in our own convenient manner. We participate when it does not conflict with our self-serving interests such as employment, vacation, business activity, hunting season, state fair, Indian rodeo, pow-wow, not having proper ceremonial paraphernalia, etc.[89]

Secakuku goes on to say that he is not criticizing anyone but is simply speaking from observation and his own personal experience. Then he continues by asking the Hopi to follow the Hopi way as instructed by the elders, for only the spiritual values of life endure forever. His final remark is a plea for Hopis to "be especially grateful for our spiritual Hopi world—therein lies the strength to overcome all that is base in our lives." The practicality of Hopi prayer acts is still recognized by Hopis as the ultimate solution to their problematical way of life.

Another example is an open letter written to Tribal Chairman Sidney by Tony Dukepoo concerning the internal problems encountered today on First Mesa. After carefully stating the possible problems presented by all parties concerned with the political leadership of First Mesa, Dukepoo humbly stated that he did not know if the solution was to be found in clan ancestral teachings or in individual self-examination, but he added in closing: "May I say that a small prayer feather and a handful of prayer meal goes a long way, more than any other thing that is known to the Hopi people. It is my prayer that we not lose sight of [that]."[90]

More recently, other Hopis have openly spoken critically about internal problems confronting Hopis. For example, for several years First Mesa has experienced a severe problem with regard to the election of Tribal Council members. The Hopi Constitution states that members must be elected from the villagers and certified by the village chief. Considerable conflict apparently exists between the Tribal Council and the village chief, for in recent years First Mesa was unable to decide on a council constituency. Several members were either elected or certified but were removed from office because they were not both elected and certified. Jimmie Honanie of Kikotsmovi was very somber in October 1982 at a meeting concerning the decertification of several elected officials at First Mesa by the village chief. He stated that appreciation and respect seemed to be absent among the Hopi and that "we only cover ourselves with the name 'Hopi,' beneath that cover, we don't practice the true meaning of being Hopi."[91]

The Hopi newspaper *Qua'Töqti* has reported many of the internal problems confronting the authenticity of Hopi religious experience. For instance, the editor, Abbot Sekaquaptewa, noted that fields were often neglected and became overrun by weeds. According to him, the problem of field neglect was pervasive, and thus he asked rhetorically, "What are we ready and willing to do to reverse the decline of the Hopi way?"[92] The editor also wrote that youth basketball practice often interfered with kiva teachings in the winter and that Hopis were no longer quiet during the December moon when the generative forces of life were at work.[93] A member of the Hopi Athletic Association pointed out that his recreational organization schedules winter events around the ceremonial calendar and that other groups should do the same.[94]

Qua'Töqti reported that in February 1983 a Santa Claus was seen on First Mesa distributing gifts during the Powamuya ceremony.[95] Furthermore, Hopi kachinas were seen in various villages during American holidays, such as Easter, Father's Day, and Mother's Day.[96] Not only do kachinas sometimes dance at nontraditional times; they also fail to distribute gifts appropriate to the sacred concerns of life, warmth, fertility, and moisture. Many Hopis think the changes in kachina dances reflect the decline of Hopi religion; others think they are representative of religious fusion and incorporation.

Hopi elders often speak of former days, when sacred rains came more regularly than they do now because the ancestors followed the Hopi path more closely.[97] Talayesva would add that Hopis were also healthier in the not-so-distant past and lived longer lives. His point is interesting, for recently a member of the Indian Health Service wrote of the great advances in health care among Hopis.[98] Any advances in Hopi health and longevity, of course, must be viewed against the background of diseases such as smallpox and alcoholism that were nonexistent before the arrival of whites. In other words, Hopis today may be healthier than they were during the smallpox epidemics of the nineteenth century but not healthier than they were aboriginally–especially since their biggest health problem, alcoholism, can be linked to the problems of modernity.[99] True, sanitation conditions have improved, but the high altitude and sunny arid skies of Hopi have always checked disease. As for other health problems, such as smallpox, the Indian Health Service has done no more than help solve problems that white people initiated.

That is not to condemn the Indian Health Service, however, for it does its best to provide health care to the Hopi. But to be adequately cared for the Hopi need better health care facilities and more Hopi health workers. An editorial in *Qua'Töqti* by Caren Coor, director of the Hopi Health Manpower Development Program, asked interested Hopis to get involved in the health field to help their own people.[100] That may be facilitated by the Tribal Council's approval of a Hopi scholarship fund. The Hopi also are developing a proposal to build a new health care complex on First Mesa on land donated by the Horn clan.[101] If approved and built, this complex will feature nursing home facilities so that elderly Hopi will not have to be placed in units far from the reservation, in Gallup, Flagstaff, or Phoenix.

In the meantime the Hopi face a number of other internal problems. Theft appears to be on the rise at Hopi based on personal reports from Hopis and incidents about which I have read in *Qua'Töqti*. I am not talking about the theft of sacred objects but rather of everyday things such as shoes, commercial art works, even postal equipment.[102] *Qua'Töqti* has related several incidents in which Hopis have been angered by disrespectful and improper behavior at a number of ceremonies, after which the writer subtly criticized those offended for not having the good heart to forgive the wrongdoers.[103] Some residents of Bacavi were critical of certain Hotevillans for denying them access to electricity in the name of traditionalism when the Hotevillans in question in fact use electricity themselves.[104]

A problem has arisen on Second Mesa between the Tribal Council and clan leaders from the village of Mishongnovi. The problem concerns proposed federal housing on Mishongnovi lands, which has been approved by the Tribal Council, Chairman Sidney, the executive director of the Hopi Tribal Housing Authority, and Stanley Honanie, chairman of the Board of Commissioners. However, concerned Hopis Emerson Susunkewa, Neilson Honyaktewa, Wayne Susunkewa, Douglass Coochwytewa, Will Mase, and Marilyn Harris claim that Mishongnovi has no constitution and thus is not under the control of the Tribal Council. They argue that it is still under the traditional form of leadership and that they have never given permission for homes to be built on their lands. Filing a complaint in Hopi Tribal Court on March 12, 1984, the representatives of Mishongnovi tried without success to obtain a restraining order to halt construction. The plaintiffs argued against construction, saying that "this land is sacred to the clans of the village of Mishongnovi and the proposed housing will render the land unfit for the necessary sacred ceremonies of the clans, which ceremonies are necessary to the very existence of the clans and people of the village."[105]

When plastic water pipes were put in place to begin construction on March 19, 1984, Emerson Susunkewa, Wayne Susunkewa, and Neilson Honyaktewa, all religious leaders of the Sand clan, set fire to the pipes and watched them burn.[106] They said they had no other choice, since the legal system had ruled against their attempt to prevent construction on ceremonial lands. No charges were filed, and the contractor decided to move the pipeline north of the Sand clan land. He also agreed to fill in the ditches that were dug for placement of the pipes. This incident is a good example of late twentieth-century tensions between traditional Hopi religion and economic development.

Six

Sacred and Human

The Hopi do not always respect the earth as they were taught to do in the "long ago" by Maasaw. A recent editorial in *Qua'Töqti* by R. E. Carolin of the Hopi Land Operations Office stated that some Hopis using the joint use areas of their reservation were not respecting the land.[1] He wrote of severe overgrazing that has resulted in wind and water erosion due to loss of ground cover. The motive for overgrazing is, of course, to make more money in the short term, a clearly nontraditional value. All Hopis Carolin interviewed agreed that something should be done about the problem, though none wanted to lose any profits. It should be noted that the Hopi are a poor people and must earn sufficient wages to keep their land and exist within the larger American society. It may be, at least in some instances, that Hopis violate traditional values of respect for the earth in order to subsist somewhat independently and autonomously within the United States. At the same time, systematic overgrazing will only hurt the Hopi in the long term, economically and spiritually.

Hopis have displayed from time to time since their emergence improper behavior and are quick to admit they are not perfect creatures. As several Hopi elders told Harold Courlander, a man with many years of association with the Hopi, "we are not perfect yet, but through good behavior we are trying to become Hopi."[2] The term *Hopi* is translated by Emory Sekaquaptewa as "one who follows the path" and by Hopi elder Peter Nuvamsa as "one who walks in the right direction."[3] Hopi is an ideal to be striven for and periodically realized, but everyone in this world veers from the path from time to time.

The Hopi recognize their humanity, their finitude, as having been given to them in the "ancient time ago" when they emerged to this world. Indeed, Hopi mythology tells of the Hopi being led to this world by a "clown" *(tsuku)*, who, just prior to the emergence, hollered in a clown voice, saying that the Hopi would clown their way through life, pretending to be the spiritual beings they are not.[4] The Hopi in several villages still perform clown rituals *(tsuklalwa)* in conjunction with the summer kachina dances where they display the major vices of humanity, such as gluttony, selfishness, ignorance, jealousy, disrespect, and arrogance.

The rite begins in a very solemn atmosphere with kachinas dancing in the plaza for rain, crops, long life, and health. The kachinas symbolize the perfect spiritual beings that the Hopi become after death. All of a sudden a chorus of loud yells comes from one of the rooftops of the houses surrounding the dance plaza, and four clowns appear. The clowns then attempt to get down from the rooftop to the plaza. This act symbolizes the metamorphosis that occurs at death, when the spirit of a Hopi returns to the underworld below. The clowns, owing to their shortcomings as mortals, experience great difficulty as they attempt to climb down into the spiritual realm, revealing their unreadiness to become perfect beings. Once they get down into the plaza the clowns immediately demonstrate greed by attempting to claim kachinas for themselves. When the kachinas, who ignore the clowns, leave the plaza between dances, the clowns perform a number of skits that never fail to bring swarms of laughter from the observing crowd.

In 1985 I witnessed a clown skit in Kikotsmovi in which the clowns performed a "graduation ceremony" at Northern Arizona University. The university is located near the Hopi reservation in Flagstaff, Arizona, and is attended by several Hopis. The clown graduates satirized graduating Hopis, who expressed tearful joy at their accomplishment. The point of the performance seemed clear: many Hopi youths today take more pride in accomplishments in the white world than they do in living a life of Hopi.

The clowns are indeed very funny in their own right, but there is a deeper underlying meaning to the laughter they evoke from onlookers. By representing the Hopi people, the clowns portray contemporary shortcomings and limitations; thus when the people laugh at the clowns, they also laugh at themselves. The clown ceremony thereby serves to remind the Hopi of their own problems, some of which are specifically Hopi and some of which are inherent in all humans.

The clown ceremony lasts two days. On the afternoon of the second day, various Whipper kachinas begin to come into the plaza where the clowns are. At first they talk to the clowns and warn them to change their foolish ways. The Whippers return several times and each time increase their warnings to the clowns. Later still, the Owl kachina enters the plaza. Owl kachina, who symbolizes the conscience of the Hopi, throws small stones at the clowns to disturb them. The stones represent the pangs of Hopi conscience, which strike when Hopis do not act right. The clowns, however, refuse to change their behavior until the Whippers purify them with the sting of yucca blade whips, followed by a water bath. Only then do the clowns become responsible for their actions.

Clowning itself embodies a sacred dimension, for the Hopi emerged as clowns in the long ago. In a sense, all Hopis are descendants of the original clown youth and clown maiden. Clowning symbolizes the sacredness of humanity in the strict sense—that there is something sacred in being a finite and mortal being separated from god. Though the goal of the Hopi way is to cultivate one's spiritual essence as much as possible in order to be perfect, that aim is perceived as impossible to fulfill in this world. It is only in the next world, when Hopis become pure spirit, that they can transcend their humanity. Of course, this is not to say that Hopis simply accept their human frailties and treat them as sacred, because the conscience, the spark of the sacred, is always present, reminding them of how they should be.

It is too simplistic to say that the Hopi are no longer traditional because they do not always follow the Hopi law of life (hopivötskwani). It may be true that as a people they stray from the Hopi path more than they once did, but clearly they have maintained at least the memory of and nostalgia for those earlier days, if not the periodic embodiment of the principles of the "long ago." Besides, their failure to be Hopi is itself sacred, for all Hopis imitate the original clown ancestors by and through their weaknesses and limitations. In that sense, the Hopi treat the finitude of humanity as sacred, thereby understanding even greed and ignorance to have a timeless dimension.

As this study has shown, the Hopi have known change since they first began settling Black Mesa, giving up their meandering, migratory pattern of orientation. But the Hopi are still wandering within their sacred land; as one Hopi said, "we are still settling our land, for new villages continue to be established."[5] It seems to me that the issue is not whether or not the Hopi have changed, but rather the way in which they have done so. The Hopi themselves resist the idea that they are a timeless, anachronistic people, as whites have often romanticized them.[6] Nevertheless, for the most part they perceive their own history of change as one that has preserved their constitutive religious values. Whether their changes have been motivated internally or externally, through peaceful exchange or contact with a dominant culture, the Hopi by and large feel that they have done what has been evoked by the world in order to sustain their relationship with the enduring rhythms of their sacred environment. Harry James's remarks are insightful:

> Their history indicates not only an exceptional ability to change but also a willingness to take time to discriminate and reflect before abandoning the old for the new. Even today the Hopi are much more likely to reckon time by the stately march of the sun across the far reaches of the desert sky than by the quick second tick of a clock. Possibly this is why they can take the long view of events tending to shape their lives.[7]

Although the Hopi have been forced to make some changes in the twentieth century, I showed in the preceding chapter that they have tried to compartmentalize those changes, viewing them as necessary for dealing harmoniously and fruitfully with a dominant society. Furthermore, they simultaneously perceive some of those forced changes as prophesied since the beginning and hence as paradoxically fulfilling the Hopi plan of life by presaging the final day of purification, when all evil will be overcome. It is this last understanding that is especially troubling to Hopis, for prophetic understandings of the contemporary world might become fatalistic and, in the end, self-fulfilling. To combat the fatalistic understanding of prophecy, the Fourth Annual Hopi Mental Health Conference chose happiness, health, and peace as its theme, focusing on "the future of the Hopi with the purpose of enhancing each individual's outlook to the coming years in a positive fashion rather than with despair or skepticism."[8]

Hopi prophecy is poorly understood and not well documented. It is not clear whether prophecies traditionally flourished among the Hopi or paralleled white cultural contact in the late nineteenth and twentieth centuries. There is, furthermore, no orthodox interpretation of Hopi prophecy, for it is a very complex phenomenon. Most Hopis agree, however, that a proper understanding of prophecy does not lead to a fatalistic view of Hopi destiny but serves as a tool for spiritual growth and the "betterment of others."[9] Hopi prophecy forecasts a number of possibilities that may or may not come to pass. Furthermore, prophecy holds that all those future possibilities exist because they have occurred before in previous worlds. I think it was the realization of that fact that led Benjamin Whorf to argue that "the Hopi language contains no reference to 'time,' either explicit or implicit."[10] The Hopi, like all humans, are aware of historical duration, as shown by C. F. Voegelin and by Ekkehart Malotki.[11] I think that Whorf was correct, however, in asserting the timeless character of Hopi religious consciousness. While it is true, as Whorf himself first noted,[12] that within the cosmic cycles the Hopi perceive time as a process of becoming later and later, ultimately the history of becoming is engulfed by the "long ago." Indeed, it seems strange that Whorf and later R. Maitland Bradfield failed to realize that the Hopi perception of time as a process of making the unmanifest manifest must be understood within cycles of time that are atemporal. In other words, the Hopi experience nothing new religiously, for all that will occur has occurred before.

Emory Sekaquaptewa has said that Hopi prophecy implies neither absolute freedom nor fatalism for the Hopi people. According to him, prophecy outlines numerous paths of life, and the Hopi are granted some freedom to decide which path they will traverse in this world.[13] Nonetheless, recalling the Hopi emergence myth, he adds that each possibility was realized in a previous world, and thus none was truly new. Or, as Abbot Sekaquaptewa said, "all these things that are predicted to happen already happened in the previous world."[14] Prophecy is a very important part of following the Hopi way. It forecasts various positive possibilities that assist the Hopi in attempting to deal more meaningfully with a changing world but also ultimately justifies negative events that disrupt the Hopi way. In other words, prophecy helps give the Hopi the strength to seek positive solutions to various problems as well as the strength to endure crises and negative events. Some Hopis summed up prophetic understanding this way:

> Prophecy provides one with a strong direction in life. It illustrates definite patterns of evolution in this world, lets individuals know what to expect for the future, and as such prepares them for the inevitable. By taking note of prophecy and recognizing the signs of its fulfillment, people can adjust their lives in accordance with the ways of the universe, and by doing so, prolong the existence of this world. There is a definite strength in prophecy: it provides a clear recognition of present-day realities, it calls for an acceptance of disharmony and corruption in spirit, and it points towards the importance of self-sufficiency, self-discipline, and attentiveness to Hopi teachings and practices in preparation for the next world.
>
> Unfortunately, few Hopis appear to be taking note of prophecy and adjusting their lives for the better. . . . Most people express frustration and depression when talking about prophecy. . . .
>
> Prophecy has been used as an excuse to avoid personal responsibility in improving the qualities of life and behaving in a way that follows Hopi teachings and beliefs. There runs a tremendous pessimism throughout Hopi that things will only get worse. This has immobilized a great deal of the population to either watch life deteriorate from a distance, or join in on the fun and go downhill as well. . . . As such Hopi prophecy becomes a self-fulfilling prophecy—the people help to make it happen sooner. . . .
>
> It is foretold that although this world will end, no one can predict exactly when this event will come to pass. In the meantime, people have lives to lead and a responsibility to do their utmost to contribute to the harmony of the universe—and other peoples' well-being.[15]

Thus Hopi prophecy asks that each Hopi do his or her best in following the precepts of the Hopi way while justifying the end of traditional practices as part of the prophesied end of the world. Therefore, prophecy allows the Hopi to view their rapidly changing contemporary situation as meaningful in the end.

All prophecies of the end of the fourth world are in some way related to the coming of whites. Given the Hopi's freedom to follow a number of predetermined paths, there are a number of prophecies regarding whites, all of which the Hopi claim have existed since the beginning.[16] All prophecies surrounding the whites are eschatological or messianic in character. In all versions, despite their differences, the return of the older brother of the Hopi will mark the end of the fourth world Hopi plan of life,[17] at which time all evil will be purified.

One tradition, as I related earlier, holds that after emerging together with the Hopi, the white brother migrated east with half of a sacred stone tablet that matches a half held by the Fire clan on Third Mesa.[18] The prophecy states that the Hopi await the return of the "true white brother" who holds the matching sacred tablet, at which time the Hopi will sit down with the whites and become as one people.

Many versions of Hopi prophecy differentiate between the whites who have already arrived at Hopi and the prophesied white man who has yet to return.[19] As I discussed earlier, the prophecy most widespread today on Third Mesa holds that the Hopi are now being confronted by whites who offer the Hopi both good and evil in order to test the purity of their hearts. The Hopi should discriminate carefully between all that is being offered and accept only that which is good for the Hopi, that is, consonant with constitutive, underlying values of the Hopi way. When the prophesied white man catches up with the Hopi, he will see whether the Hopi are true to their ancient teachings and practices. If not, he will shake a Hopi by the ear, and the Hopi people will then become like him and live his way of life. If, however, the Hopi are found to have been true to their traditions, the white brother will go to an ash heap and kick an old shoe. Then he and all other whites will become Hopis. The Hopi therefore postulate that all people will become one at the end of the world, the character of that unity being dependent upon the prophesied path the Hopi choose to take.

At first glance it may seem as though Hopi prophecy is itself ethnocentric, since the goal is for everyone to become Hopi. But it must be remembered that Hopi means "one who follows the path" or "one who walks in the right direction." A Hopi is one who seeks proper relationship with all aspects of the world. In other words, Hopi is a classification that is more spiritual than biological. The Hopi often refer to themselves as a "chosen" people, but it is a distinction that fosters unity and universality. It is more important to look at deeds than at words when investigating ethnocentrism, and an examination of Hopi history reveals a people who feel chosen to the extent necessary to live meaningful lives. And therein lies a paradox. The Hopi experience unity with humanity through their divisions of clan, village, and tribe. By contrast, Western peoples spend much effort talking about human unity, which they seek to promote by constructing global mechanisms that in reality fragment humanity. Bureaucracy, industry, communications, economics, and scientific technology have arguably increased rather than decreased the divisiveness of the human community. The Hopi talk division but live unity; the West talks unity but lives division.

It is possible to say that in the past century the Hopi have undergone qualitative changes that seem to mark the demise of the Hopi way of life. Such was the conclusion of Richard Brandt, who noted that traditional values of frugality and hard work were rapidly diminishing among the Hopi.[20] Yet a lucid awareness of many traditional values remains intact, even if they are not always embodied. As Emory Sekaquaptewa stated, "But even now, it is apparent that the Hopi people are still clinging, however little, to these ways of traditional knowledge. Because it is a deep-rooted thing, it will sprout for us again in yet other ways."[21] Even Hopis who leave the reservation to work in the cities feel the loss of the spiritual tranquillity that life on the reservation affords them, and almost all who leave desire to return eventually.[22]

The Hopi may temporarily have loosened their grip on certain religious perceptions and patterns of behavior, but they have not lost sight of them completely. The end of the fourth world is not yet here, and the Hopi seem to feel that it is still possible to restore to the world traditional values and orientations that may have been forgotten due to dominance or negligence and that it is also possible to continue to embody other teachings and practices that have remained constant. In 1981 a young Hopi from Sichomovi told me that although the Hopi today use a number of Western techniques and tools, the core of the traditional ways of being are still known so that the Hopi could survive tomorrow if they lost all knowledge and use of Western technology, a point echoed in *Qua'Töqti* in 1984.[23] Emory Sekaquaptewa wrote that the Hopi, as individuals, accept the need for understanding many ways of the whites but as a people are concerned with living traditional Hopi values.[24] For example, when Alph Secakuku was appointed superintendent of the Bureau of Indian Affairs Hopi Agency, he said he would work legally for policies of self-determination yet admitted that as a Hopi certain of his clan duties would not change.[25]

In 1951 some chiefs and various clan and religious society members in Shongopavi drew up a statement that was presented to the commissioner of Indian affairs. This statement outlined the traditional boundaries of Hopiland and clearly demonstrated the religious character of the Hopi way of life. It also reflected these Hopis' continued knowledge and support of Hopi traditions and brought home the point that for the Hopi, their land, life, and religion are one:

> The Hopi Tusqua is our Love and will always be, and it is the land upon which our leader fixes and tells the dates for our religious life. Our land, our religion, and our life are one, and our leader, with humbleness, understanding and determination, performs his duty to us by keeping them as one and thus insuring prosperity and security for the people.
> 1. It is from the land that each true Hopi gathers the rocks, the plants, the different woods, roots, and his life, and each in the authority of his rightful obligation brings to our ceremonies proof of our ties to this land. Our footprints mark well the trails to these sacred places where each year we go in performance of our duties.
> 2. It is from this land that we have hunted and were assured of

rights to game such as deer, elk, antelope, buffalo, rabbit, turkey. It is here that we captured the eagle, hawk, and such birds whose feathers belong to our ceremonies.

3. It is upon this land that we made trails to our salt supply.

4. It is over this land that many people have come seeking places for settlement, and . . . asked our leader for permission to settle in this area. All the clan groups named their contributions to our welfare and upon acceptance by our leader were given designated lands for their livelihood and for their eagle hunting, according to the directions from which they came.

5. It is from this land that we obtained the timbers and stone for our homes and kivas.

6. It is here on this land that we are bringing up our younger generation and through preserving the ceremonies are teaching them proper human behavior and strength of character to make them true citizens among all people.

7. It is upon this land that we wish to live in peace and harmony with our friends and with our neighbors.[26]

It is true that some ceremonies have been forgotten, game is scarce, salt is usually purchased at a grocery store, houses are commonly built of cinder block, and children often drag out their traditional education by spending time away from home. Nevertheless, it is still fair to say that the Hopi are very religious in a Hopi way. All of these changes are related to their being dominated by another society. Most are forced upon them, though some may be the result of acquiescence. Whether contemporary Hopi changes are compartmentalized or accepted ultimately as prophesied, however, they are by and large necessary for the survival of the Hopi. It seems to me that human beings are multidimensional and that the Hopi must relate realistically to their subordinate situation. Whether they can continue to compartmentalize their lives in order to preserve their constitutive religious values and behavior while relating harmoniously to whites remains to be seen. I do know that the Hopi are a persistent and persevering people who revere their land and life. As Andrew Hermequaftewa stated, "The Hopiland is the Hopi religion. The Hopi religion is bound up in the Hopiland."[27] Indeed, Abbot Sekaquaptewa has said that "without our land, we are nothing."[28]

The Hopi cannot simply go back and restore the times of their ancestors, as they themselves are fully aware. Nevertheless, they refuse to acquiesce fully to the dominant influences of white Americans. At the same time, once such influences arrive they can accept them as prophesied and go ahead positively from there. Although they willingly though cautiously accept some positive aspects of the Western world, they do not simply say that all Western influence is consonant with the Hopi way. In other words, the Hopi experience a powerful tension in their lives today, as do all oppressed peoples who are attempting to live an authentically religious life.

In 1982 the Hopi proposed a land assignment ordinance that would provide for the possibility of commercial development on Hopi partitioned lands.[29] The purpose was to promote economic self-determination so that the Hopi would be less reliant on white Americans. It has been estimated that the Hopi spend at least 60 percent of their earnings off the reservation, most of it in non-Hopi grocery stores in Flagstaff.[30] This same desire for self-determination is behind the Hopi's development of a high school, a medical complex, a proposed shopping mall with grocery store, laundromat, restaurant, auto parts store, discount store, drug store, dry cleaner, entertainment center, and bank. The desire for self-determination is also behind the development of a number of agencies that provide jobs for Hopis on the reservation.[31] At the same time, the proposed ordinance stated that commercial development must not damage any sacred springs and that no usage could restrict or limit the use of the land for subsistence and traditional gathering of fuel, plants, or other materials by members of the Hopi tribe. Thus, in principle, economic self-sufficiency and traditional religiosity were both promoted.

All the problems the Hopi face today are their own, of course, therefore non-Hopi views (including my own) concerning solutions matter little, if at all, to the Hopi people. I have simply tried to understand and communicate to those interested the Hopi's current situation in a way that does some justice to their own experience. The Hopi are not interested as a people in impressing non-Hopis that they are a genuinely religious people, for their problem is one of strengthening their own cultural and religious values in order to strengthen themselves.[32] To do otherwise is to define their identity in terms of the values of the dominant society, thereby acceding to the very dominance they wish to dissolve.

By and large the Hopi have not accepted the stereotypes attributed to them by whites, and indeed, a number of Hopis have made it clear that they reject the interpretations of them by non-Hopis. The Hopi are beginning to respond critically to a number of interpretive studies in light of their own traditional teachings and are making it clear that they will not accept definitions of themselves by those who are part of the dominant society.[33] That, I think, is good and has led me on more than one occasion to question the presuppositions and conclusions of my own work. The Hopi do not mind being studied as humans, but they have reservations about those who study them in order to claim expertise in Hopi studies.[34] It is my opinion that outsiders are able at times to perceive aspects of Hopi life of which Hopis themselves may be unaware (the same is true conversely). The Hopi are not fond of scholars who examine them in order to acquire status in the dominant society, especially since the Hopi have no real power to decide and determine what gets published and what is considered good or bad. There is a need for true human dialogue in Hopi studies today, but one must ask whether that can occur as long as the Hopi are a subordinate people. What, then, is the proper locus of Hopi studies today?

The Hopi in 1984 attempted to put together an ordinance that would, in part, allow the Hopi to "control all documentation of all studies of the tribe, its villages, people, lands and environment, and culture and traditions." Milland Lomakema was appointed cultural preservation specialist and was to be in charge of organizing this new ordinance, whose overall purpose was to "control the conduct of persons visiting the reservation so as to protect artifacts and religious artifacts."[35] Unfortunately, Lomakema was unable to acquire sufficient funding to enact this plan, and so it was tabled. The very possibility of implementing such a plan presupposed both financial help and political approval from the very society from which the Hopi need protection. Such irony illuminates rather profoundly the fundamental quandary facing the Hopi today as they wrestle with the problems of being subjected to domination.

I am reminded of a Hopi folk tale in which the structural changes effected by the presence of white Americans are clearly depicted. A Hopi man was visiting the ancestral ruins at Kawestima in what is now Navajo country. Looking off in the distance he noticed two persons approaching who appeared to be Navajo. Fearing for his life, he jumped down into an old kiva, hoping he had not been spotted. He was, however, seen by the two men, who were in fact white tourists. They were curious about the behavior of the Hopi and thought that perhaps they might witness some secret Hopi ceremony. They approached the kiva and looked in at the Hopi, who was quite surprised to see that the men were not Navajo after all. The tourists then asked the surpised Hopi the purpose of his action. Trying to recover his composure and wanting to impress his visitors, the Hopi responded, "I am here because of you and you are here because of me."

This story summarizes in narrative form the situation in which the Hopi find themselves today. They cannot understand themselves apart from their subjection to white Americans, who likewise cannot understand themselves apart from their dominant relationship with the Hopi and other Native Americans. Each group presupposes the other in ways unknown to either group prior to contact.[36] The Hopi find themselves today in a historically unique religious situation. The study of Hopi religion is a study of religion in America or religion in the New World.[37] In America, peoples from diverse backgrounds and religions met. Those encounters changed all parties. In one sense, it is no longer accurate to talk about Hopis and whites, and not just because race is never static. Neither is spirit. Hopis and Westerners met and became transformed. Both are in a new world that is neither Hopi nor Western, but rather one where each is part of the other's world.

And yet this unique existential situation is simultaneously understood by the Hopi as the fulfillment of prophecy. In this sense the Hopi's subjection to a dominant society is understood as an event prophesied in the "long ago" that also occurred in other previous worlds. The contemporary Hopi religious orientation embodies this ambivalent and paradoxical experience of white American domination.

The Hopi cosmogony describes the birth of the Hopi in a way homologous to the growth of plants. The germination of the Hopi people, like that of the corn that defines them, does not signify a break with the world. The Hopi remain rooted in the source of their emergence. In religious terms, the Hopi experience the "very something" as distant yet related. That is the paradox of the Hopi way of life.

Notes

Full details of references are in the annotated bibliography.

Introduction

1. F. Eggan 1950, pp. 87–88.
2. Hough 1918a, pp. 71 and 132.
3. Interviewed in Shorris 1971, p. 132.
4. Kalectaca 1978, pp. 190–92.
5. See Whorf 1950, p. 69 n. 2.
6. W. James 1958, p. 61; Otto 1923.
7. See Jones 1905; Fletcher 1910; Hewitt 1901; Lamphere 1969, p. 282; Lowie 1922, p. 315; Boas, 1948, pp. 612–13; and Mooney 1972, p. 518.
8. O'Kane 1950, p. 206.
9. Kennard 1972, p. 470.
10. H. James 1974, pp. 102–3; Page 1982b, pp. 216–17.
11. Whiteley 1988a.
12. The phenomenon of compartmentalization is treated more fully in chapter five.

Part I. Work and Ritual

One. A Religious Practicality

1. This concept of timeless experience through repetition of ancestral patterns of behavior was developed in the history of religions by Eliade 1954, p. 32, and 1969, preface and p. 28. The Hopi refer to their mythical ancestors as "people of long ago" (*hisatsinom*).

2. Charles Long labeled these existential and cosmic modes as ordinary and extraordinary respectively (personal communication).

3. Sometimes the Hopi also refer to mythic time as "long ago" (*hisat*). Malotki 1983b, p. 663 n. 193, noted that in precontact times the Hopi also referred to mythic time by the designation "incredibly many" (*soomori*), but after contact with whites the Hopi became increasingly conscious of historical time and translated *soomori* as "one thousand."

4. *Sipaapuni* refers to the Hopi place of origin and emergence to this world. A highly symbolic term, it seems not to break down into any component parts. "Navel" (*sipna*) seems to be the basic etymon. Some

Hopis have suggested that *sipaapu* is a distortion of *sipna*, since both are related to birth. Apparently the term is so significant that it is highly symbolic and numinous, hiding the ordinary word *sipna*. As some Hopis say, "by means of it, it will be concealed, that's why" *(put akw pam pay tupkiwtaniqw oovi'o)*. Emory Sekaquaptewa, to whom I am indebted for this explication, further transliterates: "The concealment makes it obscure or unexplainable." Here is shown an example of a religious term whose sacredness is manifested by its ineffable character. Religiously, this makes sense in that religious symbols point to universal and timeless meanings, meanings not bound by place or duration.

5. O'Kane 1953, p. 177; see also O'Kane 1950, p. 208. A number of studies have addressed the relationship between work and ritual. See Elkin et al. 1950, pp. 3–4; Wach 1951, pp. 30–47; Long 1967; Bordieu 1977; Hultkrantz 1965, 1966, 1974, and 1976; Gill 1982, pp. 32–34, 1976, p. 32, 1977–78, and 1981; Vecsey, 1980; Fickeler 1962; and Rappaport 1979.

6. The Hopi diet has changed since World War II; see Kennard 1965. Hotevilla is unique in harvesting more beans than corn because it lacks floodwater plots, which are ideal for corn.

7. For an important recent discussion of Maasaw's link to Hopi agriculture, see Malotki and Lomatuway'ma 1987b, chap. 6.

8. See Beaglehole 1937, pp. 33–49; Curtis 1970, pp. 41–43; Forde 1931; and Titiev 1938 and 1944a, pp. 181–87.

9. Curtis 1970, p. 41.

10. Titiev 1938, p. 41. See also Malotki 1983b, pp. 471–73.

11. Titiev 1944a, p. 184.

12. Whiteley 1985 and 1986 argued that the Hopi do not have clan lands; rather, they have ceremonial fields *(wimvaavasa)* whose basis is more religious than social. I agree. At the same time, it is fair to say that the Hopi regularly experience lands as clan owned. That does not mean they experience lands as more social than religious, for clans carry much religious experience. That Whiteley notes many incongruities between Hopi clan land theory and practice does not mean such gaps are experienced by the Hopi. A distinguishing feature of ritual practice is the way in which insiders see harmony between theory and practice where outsiders see conflict; see Jonathan Z. Smith, "The Bare Facts of Ritual," *History of Religions* 20 (1980–81): 112–27.

13. The planter traditionally works from the south side of the field to the north side. "Once someone did it north to south but was stopped," said one Hopi, clearly demonstrating the importance of religious custom. See Breunig and Lomatuway'ma 1983, p. 5.

14. Beaglehole 1937, p. 39.

15. Wallis 1936, p. 10; Whiting 1939, pp. 11 and 40–41.

16. Bradfield 1971.

17. E. Sekaquaptewa 1976, p. 42.

18. E. Richard Hart, "Historic Zuni Land Use," *Zuni History*, Zuni, N.M.: Zuni History Project and Institute of American West, 1983, p. 5.

19. Stewart and Nicholson 1940, p. 47.

20. Talayesva 1942, p. 229. But even a greasewood planting stick hurts the ground, for "digging a hole is like stabbing the ground." Thus spoke Percy Lomaquahu, Eagle clan chief from Hotevilla; see *Katsi: Happiness, Health and Peace* 1984, p. 56. That some Hopis use metal digging sticks but still insist they use wood is a good example of how mythic peoples perceive harmony where Westerners see discrepancy.

21. See Nequatewa 1967, pp. 24–27; Stephen 1929, pp. 7–10, and 1936, pp. 150–51; Voth 1905b, pp. 13 and 16–26; and Malotki and Lomatuway'ma 1987b, chap. 4.

22. Toelken 1976, p. 14.

23. Several oral traditions mention Maasaw's gifts to the Hopi; see Courlander 1982, pp. 4–5; Nequatewa 1967, p. 26; Stephen 1929, p. 55; Voth 1905b, p. 13; Fewkes and Stephen 1892, p. 196; and Malotki and Lomatuway'ma 1987b.

24. Stephen 1936, pp. 150–51.

25. Maasaw seems to be associated in some way with Muy'ingwa, the god of germination. Bradfield 1973, pp. 254–58, rightly stated that Maasaw's realm is the surface of this, the fourth world, while Muy'ingwa's abode is the underworld. As I argued elsewhere (Loftin 1983, pp. 300–302, and 1986, pp. 182 and 186) all Hopi deities are understood as cosmic rhythms and forms. Thus Maasaw is death (in one sense), and Muy'ingwa is germination. In other words, Maasaw is present wherever and whenever there is death, Muy'ingwa wherever and whenever there is life. Or, more specifically, Maasaw reveals himself in the metamorphosis from life to death, while Muy'ingwa manifests himself in the metamorphosis from death to life. This interpretation accounts for the separate realms of Maasaw (surface) and Muy'ingwa (underworld), as well as their inseparable relationship.

26. Scott Momaday, a Kiowa, made a similar statement about Native Americans as a whole; see Momaday 1976, p. 84.

27. Brown 1976, p. 27.

28. Deloria 1973, p. 270, and 1970, p. 197. I want to emphasize that this idea reflects Deloria's view several years ago. I mention it here only to help make a point.

29. Overholt 1979, p. 16.

30. Capps 1976, p. 113.

31. Long 1963, p. 18; see also Long 1980.

32. *Qua'Töqti: The Eagle's Call*, Sept. 23, 1982, p. 4.

Two. A Sacred Society

1. Eliade 1958, p. 38.

2. Ortiz 1972, p. 143.

3. Malotki gave a number of terms to refer to the Hopi supreme being (which he said is now Maasaw), including *i'himu qataymataq qatuuga*, "this being that lives unseen," and *i'hikwsit himuy'taqa*, "the one who has the breath." See Malotki and Lomatuway'ma 1987b, p. 248. Lomatuway'ma

said the concept of *hiita*, the "someone" deity, whom Geertz called the "supreme deity," is sometimes referred to as *hikwsit himuy'taqa*, "one who gives (or has) breath." See Geertz and Lomatuway'ma 1987, p. 68 n. 18.

4. Whorf 1950, p. 69 n. 2.

5. See Kennard 1972, p. 471; Malotki 1983a, pp. 25–28; and Courlander 1982, p. 101.

6. E. Sekaquaptewa 1976, p. 38; Gill 1977.

7. See Loftin 1983, pp. 300–308, and 1986.

8. The term *refraction* is taken from E. E. Evans-Pritchard, *Nuer Religion*, Oxford: Oxford University Press, 1956, p. 107.

9. Titiev 1944a, pp. 273 and 55. There is confusion concerning the relation of the term *wu'ya* to *naatoyla*. Malotki thinks *naatoyla* means "mark of one's clan," whereas Voegelin says *naatoyla* is used only in relation to phratries. For a discussion of this problem see Geertz and Lomatuway'ma 1987, p. 138, n. 80. Emory Sekaquaptewa told me in August 1988 that he defines *wu'ya* as "mythical clan ancestor," while *naatoyla* means "clan totem." *Totem* is defined simply as a clan emblem that symbolizes one's ancestry. A Hopi clan has one *wu'ya* but may have several *naatoyla*. The *naatoyla* are often used as sources for Hopi names.

10. Ibid., pp. 49 and 53. See also F. Eggan 1950, pp. 65–66 (Eggan's list of clans is taken from Stephen, Fewkes, Lowie, Forde, Titiev, and his own field research), and Whiteley 1985, pp. 364–65.

11. F. Eggan 1950, p. 63.

12. See Titiev 1944a, p. 55, and F. Eggan 1950, p. 82.

13. F. Eggan 1950, pp. 82 and 62.

14. Talayesva 1942, pp. 159 and 439.

15. F. Eggan 1933.

16. Hieb 1979b, p. 65.

17. See Bradfield 1973.

18. Durkheim and Mauss 1963; Lévi-Strauss 1966; Hieb 1972, p. 86; Thompson and Joseph 1944, pp. 38 and 44.

19. F. Eggan 1950, pp. 86–87. It was Eggan's insight that helped me realize the active, practical dimension of Hopi social structure.

20. Bordieu 1977, p. 120. The practicality of Hopi logic is uncovered implicitly with reference to Hopi clans in Whiteley 1985, pp. 368–72.

21. F. Eggan 1950, p. 83.

22. Bradfield 1973, p. 224.

23. F. Eggan 1950, p. 83.

24. Parsons 1933, p. 34; Courlander 1982, p. 113; Curtis 1970, p. 99.

25. Hargrave 1939, p. 208.

26. Whiting 1939, p. 63; Stephen 1936, pp. 220, 324, 370, and 439; Waters 1963, p. 247. Though Waters's work is problematic for a number of reasons, the citation here is to remarks by John Lansa, a respected Hopi elder from Oraibi.

27. Beaglehole 1937, pp. 34–35.

28. Stephen 1936, p. 782.

29. Voth 1901, pp. 76, 77, and 83.

30. Voth 1912, p. 126.

31. Earle and Kennard 1971, pp. 17 and 19.
32. Voth 1905b, p. 10; Wallis 1936, pp. 2–7; Nequatewa 1967, pp. 16–19; Stephen 1929, pp. 6–7.
33. Parsons 1933, pp. 31–32.
34. Voth 1905b, pp. 23–25.
35. Whiting 1939, p. 23.
36. F. Eggan 1950, p. 84.
37. Voth 1915, p. 76; F. Eggan 1950, p. 84; Steward 1938, p. 312.
38. Voth 1915, pp. 75–76.
39. Hough 1918b, pp. 236–37; Stephen 1936, p. 608; Steward 1938, p. 312.
40. Stephen 1936, pp. 150–51, 709, and 825; Parsons 1925, p. 77 n. 124; Beaglehole and Beaglehole 1935, p. 12; Curtis 1970, pp. 39–40; H. Sekaquaptewa 1969, p. 150; Talayesva 1942, pp. 158–61.
41. Nequatewa 1931, p. 2; Titiev 1944a, pp. 130–41; Yava 1978, pp. 74–79.
42. Fewkes 1900b, pp. 582–84.
43. Beaglehole 1937, p. 34.
44. Titiev 1944a, pp. 191–93; Stephen 1936, pp. 84 and 87 n. 1.
45. Bradfield 1973, p. 243.
46. Wallis and Titiev 1944, pl. iii.
47. Bradfield 1973, p. 243.
48. Voth 1905b, pp. 11 and 21; Yava 1978, p. 40; Talayesva 1942, p. 420.
49. Bradfield 1973, p. 243.
50. Wallis and Titiev 1944, pl. vii.
51. E. Sekaquaptewa 1979, pp. 7–8.
52. F. Eggan 1950, p. 84.
53. Bradfield 1973, p. 243.
54. Kennard 1972, p. 470.
55. See Gill 1987.
56. Schlegel 1977.
57. Stephen 1929, p. 4.
58. This discussion of Hopi hunting is taken from Titiev 1944a, p. 190; Beaglehole 1936, pp. 14–17; Curtis 1970; Stephen 1936, p. 1229; Bradfield 1973, p. 33; and Loftin 1983, pp. 164–68.
59. Talayesva 1942, pp. 158–61.
60. Nequatewa 1933, pp. 42 and 49 n. 1; Beaglehole and Beaglehole 1935, p. 44; Titiev 1944a, p. 203.
61. Nequatewa 1933, p. 51 fig. 4.
62. Titiev 1944a, p. 58.
63. F. Eggan 1950, pp. 65–66; Bradfield 1973, pp. 200–209.
64. F. Eggan 1950, p. 86.
65. Bradfield 1973, pp. 303–4.
66. Yava 1978, p. 165.
67. M. Black 1984.
68. Voth 1905a, pp. 43–61.
69. O'Kane 1950, p. 235. For another discussion of the way in which

Hopi children are likened to maturing corn plants, see Kealunohomoku 1980, pp. 59–62.

70. F. Eggan 1950, p. 48.

71. Talayesva 1942, p. 28; H. Sekaquaptewa 1969, p. 182; Beaglehole and Beaglehole 1935, p. 33; Voth 1905a, p. 49. See also the comments of Percy Lomaquahu in *Katsi: Happiness, Health and Peace* 1984, p. 52.

72. Wallis 1936, p. 9; Voth 1905b, pp. 14–15; Talayesva 1942, p. 419; H. James 1939; Courlander 1971, p. 27.

73. For descriptions of Wuwtsim in its long, initiation form, see Talayesva 1942, pp. 157–61, and Titiev 1944a, pp. 130–41. Titiev's account reflects some data gathered from Third Mesa, but he drew primarily upon these First and Second Mesa sources: Fewkes 1900, pp. 80–138; Fewkes 1895, pp. 422–58; Stephen 1892, pp. 189–221; Parsons 1923, pp. 156–87; Stephen 1938, pp. 957–93; and Steward 1931, pp. 56–59.

74. Nequatewa 1931, p. 2.

75. Talayesva 1942, p. 159; Yava 1978, pp. 74–79. See also Titiev 1944a, p. 134.

76. Kennard 1972, p. 471.

77. In the film *Hopi: Songs of the Fourth World*, 1984.

78. Kennard 1972, p. 471. Emory Sekaquaptewa translated this speech from Second Mesa dialect into Third Mesa dialect. See also M. Black 1984, p. 280.

79. A number of Hopi terms come to mind that express the opposite of *qatungwu* (matter without life). One is a ceremonial secret that is roughly translated "spiritual substance." Another, *hikwsi*, means "breath" or "soul." A third term, *soona*, or "substance of life," is often contrasted with *qatungwa*, which is sometimes described as "without *soona*." An analysis of the relationship between these terms is badly needed.

80. Stephen 1936, p. 706; see also pp. 1254–55 and 1308.

81. Wallis 1936, p. 10.

Three. The Utility of Prayer

1. Nequatewa 1931, p. 2.

2. Titiev 1944a, p. 142.

3. Whiteley 1982 and 1988a.

4. See E. Sekaquaptewa 1972, p. 247.

5. Whiteley 1983.

6. E. Sekaquaptewa 1972, p. 247.

7. *Qua'Töqti*, Sept. 16, 1982, p. 2; Nov. 24, 1982, p. 2.

8. Talayesva 1942, pp. 169–70.

9. Qoyawayma 1964, p. 86.

10. I discussed Hopi prayer acts in detail in Loftin 1986.

11. Gill 1982, p. 81.

12. The data given here on Powamuya are taken from several Third Mesa sources: Titiev 1944a, pp. 114–20; Voth 1901; Talayesva 1942, pp. 191–97; and Earle and Kennard 1971, pp. 19–40.

13. The information on ritual smoking is taken from Loftin 1986, pp. 181–85.

14. O'Kane 1953, p. 148; Means 1960, p. 121; Voth 1905b, p. 117; Stephen 1936, p. 791.

15. For a drawing of the Powamuya sand mosaic, see Voth 1901, pl. xlii.

16. The description in this paragraph is from Voth 1901, p. 76.

17. Titiev wrote that the War chief was not present during Powamuya, but Talayesva, who is from Oraibi, said that this chief was present at one point in the rite; see Titiev 1944a, p. 114 n. 30, and Talayesva 1942, p. 195.

18. Stephen 1936, p. 1305; Nequatewa 1967, p. 130 n. 40; Stephen 1929, p. 62.

19. Talayesva 1942, p. 63.

20. Stephen 1936, pp. 781–82.

21. See Talayesva 1942, pp. 163–65.

22. Wallis 1936, p. 15.

23. Ibid.; Stephen 1929, pp. 13–14.

24. Stephen 1940, p. 214, and 1929, pp. 7 and 39; Titiev 1944b, p. 428 n. 9, and 1944a, p. 123. See also Fewkes and Stephen 1893, p. 276. There is no one Hopi deity who is "mother earth." *Tuwapongtumsi* (Sand Altar Maiden) comes closest, perhaps, though she seems to be especially mother of all plants. *Tiikuywuuti* (Child Sliding Out Woman) is mother of all game animals and *Taalawtumsi* (Dawn Woman) is goddess of childbirth who also helps look after Hopi plants. See Geertz and Lomatuway'ma 1987, p. 73. Geertz says that Hopi deities generally do not have alternative names and thus theorizes that the above are perhaps separate entities or are similar deities of different origin. That may be true, historically speaking, but it is not clear to me that the Hopi make great effort to distinguish them. Titiev claims that *Tuwapongtumsi* or *Tuwapongwuuti* (Sand Altar Woman) is identical to Tiikuywuuti and that the Hopi hunter offers prayers to either. People such as the Hopi, for whom mythic modes of understanding are dominant, often see relation, where more historically oriented people see difference; Loftin 1987.

Sam Gill's *Mother Earth* raises another issue. Gill argues that "it is unproductive to collapse the many goddesses and other figures of feminine identity into a single goddess." Gill is arguing the point at an *inter*-tribal and cross-cultural level, although I suppose he would also argue it at an *intra*-tribal level. Gill goes on to write that "though the structure of Mother Earth may be primordial and archetypal, historically this structure was not formally identified nor did it take on importance until recently, that is, within the last hundred years." My response to Gill's thesis depends on context. I agree with Christopher Vecsey when he writes, "If Gill is saying that traditional Indians believed in, and prayed to, female goddesses associated with the earth, whom they sometimes referred to as mothers, but that in the last century a more unified major Mother Earth concept has coalesced as part of inter-tribal Indian religious culture, it is plausible." That statement seems to fit the Hopi case with their many feminine goddesses. Gill does accept the possibility that the structure of

Mother Earth may be archetypal but says it was not formally identified until recently. I am not certain what he means by that remark. If he means that the earth as a symbolic mother (or even a metaphorical mother) is not an ancient and fundamental part of Native American religious consciousness, then I, like Thomas Buckley, disagree. But if Gill is saying only that the actual English term *Mother Earth* surfaces among Indian tribes in the last one hundred years, then I agree with Gill. The tougher question, it seems to me is this: is the religious meaning of the term *Mother Earth* necessarily new? In this book, I argue that Hopi religious experience simultaneously embodies structures of meaning from the precontact past and some new ones that parallel contact with Anglos. It strikes me that the term *Mother Earth* may be used by Hopis to communicate to Anglos the Hopi experience of life-giving forces. In that sense, the term is new but the meaning is old. At the same time, the term may be used by Hopis in a cross-cultural manner which carries religious meanings that parallel twentieth-century change. See Gill 1987, pp. 151–52; Vecsey 1988, p. 256; and Buckley 1989, p. 359.

25. Wallis and Titiev 1944, p. 547; Parsons 1933, p. 44; Stephen 1936, pp. xlii, 96, 147 n. 2, 318, 638, and 864.

26. Stephen 1936, pp. 306, 308, and 315.

27. Ibid., p. 1025 fig. 504.

28. Lewis 1981, p. 111. See also M. Black 1984.

29. Matthews 1888, p. 109.

30. For myths of Tiikuywuuti and Tuwapongwuuti as mothers of game, see Curtis 1970, pp. 190–93; Stephen 1936, p. 1304; Talayesva 1942, pp. 177, 228, and 426–28; and Nequatewa 1946a, pp. 61–62.

31. Bradfield 1973, p. 260.

32. Stephen 1929, pp. 18 and 51; Beaglehole 1936, pp. 17–19; Talayesva 1942, pp. 161–78.

33. Powell 1972, p. 29.

34. Voth 1901, p. 78. Bluebird feathers symbolize the arrival of both cold and warm weather because bluebirds have unique migrating habits. They arrive at Hopi in the autumn, migrating south when it turns cold, then return in spring, staying until hot weather arrives, when they move into the mountains. See Bradfield 1973, pp. 94–95.

35. Voth 1901, p. 81.

36. Ibid., p. 82.

37. I am indebted to Peter Whiteley for bringing the term *pasiuni* to my attention. *Pasiuni* is Third Mesa dialect for the Second Mesa term *pasiwna*, which Edward Kennard first noted. Whiteley translated *pasiuni* as "planning of destiny." Emory Sekaquaptewa was the first writer to mention the planned nature of the Oraibi split, but he used the term *tiingavi*, meaning "designed in deliberation." Whiteley noted Sekaquaptewa's work but said that his consultants used the term *pasiuni* rather than *tiingavi*. I asked Sekaquaptewa for clarification of the two terms and he essentially agreed with Whiteley. *Pasiuni* has applications beyond the religious and ceremonial; it can mean an ordinary plan in the secular sense. *Tiingavi* refers to something that has been preordained by priests in a formal, ceremonial

sense. It is a formal announcement accompanied by a formal smoke that sets the time for certain ceremonies. See Whiteley 1988a, p. 266; Sekaquaptewa 1972, p. 247; Kennard 1972, p. 469.

38. A great deal has been written by both Hopis and non-Hopis concerning the character and meaning of kachinas, or katsinas; they have been interpreted as gods, as supernatural intermediaries between the Hopi and the gods, and as departed ancestors. See Malotki 1983a, pp. 19–37; Kabotie 1977, p. 123; Earle and Kennard 1971, pp. 7–8 and 17; Wright 1977, pp. 2–3 and 29; Voth 1905b, p. 116; J. W. Fewkes, "Ancestor Worship of the Hopi Indians," in Smithsonian Institution Annual Report for 1921, p. 486; Titiev 1944a, p. 108 n. 43; Bradfield 1973, pp. 46–49; Stephen 1898, pp. 261–62; and Hieb 1979a, p. 577, and 1979b, p. 65.

39. Titiev 1944a, p. 114 n. 32; Wright 1977, pp. 32 and 34–35; Wright 1973, pp. 18–19.

40. Titiev 1944a, p. 115.

41. My accounts of the Powamuy and Kachina initiations are taken from these Third Mesa sources (except where otherwise noted): Earle and Kennard 1971, pp. 23–28; Talayesva 1942, pp. 79–85; Titiev 1944a, pp. 114–17; Voth 1901, pp. 88–108; E. Sekaquaptewa 1976, pp. 38–39; and H. Sekaquaptewa 1969, pp. 23–29.

42. See Wright 1979, p. 77.

43. Stephen 1898, p. 265.

44. For Tcowilawu, see Voth 1901 pl. li; Earle and Kennard 1971, p. 24; and Wright 1973, p. 70.

45. A drawing of the *poota* is in Voth 1901, p. 89 pls. li and xlviii.

46. Voth 1901, pp. 93–94.

47. For a drawing of the sand altars, see Voth 1901, p. 95 pls. lii and liii.

48. A drawing of Muy'ingwa's descent into the kiva is in Voth 1901 pl. lvii.

49. Qoyawayma 1964, p. 176.

50. The Mudhead kachinas are privileged to act somewhat as clowns; appearing at almost every dance, they also serve as singers and drummers. See Malotki 1983a, pp. 32–33; Wright 1973, p. 238; and Wright 1977, p. 48 pl. 6, and p. 78 pls. 15 and 82.

51. F. Eggan 1950, p. 432 n. 46, and pp. 49–50.

52. A list of the whips controlled by different ceremonial societies is in Titiev 1944a, p. 241.

53. Talayesva 1942, p. 193.

54. Kabotie 1977, p. 128; Malotki 1983a, pp. 38–43.

55. Titiev 1944a, p. 117.

56. Talayesva 1942, p. 193.

57. Titiev 1944a, p. 118.

58. Ibid., p. 119.

59. F. Eggan 1948, p. 372; H. Sekaquaptewa 1969, p. 29; Talayesva 1942, p. 84.

60. E. Sekaquaptewa 1976, p. 38.

61. Gill made this point in three separate works: 1976, 1977, and 1982, pp. 91–92.

62. E. Sekaquaptewa 1976, p. 39; Talayesva 1942, p. 181.

63. See Curtis 1970, p. 99, and Nequatewa 1948, p. 62. Most collections of Hopi myths do not mention the departure of the kachinas, perhaps because the tradition is told only to initiates, or because it was overlooked by Hopi consultants, or because the myth is embodied in almost mute form within the Hopi orientation to the world. The reasons given for the departure of the "real" kachinas are symbolic expressions of the mystery of human origins, not literal accounts. They are Hopi expressions of that which cannot be expressed. See Long 1967.

64. Voth 1967, p. 38. For a picture of a squash blossom headdress worn during the Bean Dance, see Wright 1979, p. 37.

65. Voth 1901, p. 71.

66. Titiev 1944a, p. 120.

67. Bradfield 1973, pp. 89–90.

68. Talayesva 1942, pp. 196–97. Similar meanings are found in Earle and Kennard 1971, pp. 23–34; O'Kane 1950, pp. 183–84; Parsons 1925, pp. 44–45; Steward 1931; and Stephen 1936, p. 156.

69. Kennard 1937, p. 491; Titiev 1944a, pp. 107, 171–73.

70. Armin Geertz, for example, wrote in 1982 (p. 188):

> I concluded that the overt aims of the ceremonials, as indicated by the symbols and actions, seem to be the procuring of rain and floods in order to bring about a good harvest. Secondly, the ceremonials transport the worshipper into the richly populated mythical and ritual time dimensions where a totality of religious desire finds the means and the modes of expressing total fulfillment.

Geertz is correct in his analysis of the twofold character of Hopi rites, but he does not address the problem of their interrelationship. He does not note that the return to the primordium is inseparably intertwined with the Hopi's concern for rain, crops, and health. To experience "again" the primordium is to recreate all cosmic forms and rhythms, which is no less than the rebirth of the world and of life itself.

71. See Eliade 1969, pp. 86–87.

72. Beaglehole and Beaglehole 1935, p. 30.

73. Wallis 1936, p. 15.

Part II. Dominance and Religion

Four. Contact and Change

1. Fred Eggan (personal communication, 1985) thinks these myths are relatively recent (post–World War II) additions to the Hopi oral tradition. Of course, myths may be embodied or lived prior to being articulated. See Leenhardt 1979; Eliade 1954.

2. Yava 1978, p. 36.

3. Qoyawayma 1964, p. 33; Cushing 1923, pp. 169–70.

4. Although the term *purification day* is used today by Hopis to describe the end of the present fourth world, I have found no evidence of its use before World War II, and Fred Eggan does not recall the term being used in the 1930s and 1940s. It may well express an archaic tradition that has now incorporated some Christian elements. See Malotki and Lomatuway'ma 1987b, pp. 247–61, for a discussion of purification day.

5. Corres 1900.

6. H. James 1974, p. 94.

7. Talayesva 1942, p. 377.

8. Jasper Poola, First Mesa, personal communication, 1980. See also Courlander 1982, pp. 10–15.

9. H. Sekaquaptewa 1969, p. 235.

10. Ibid., pp. 229 and 236.

11. Powell 1972, p. 29. Though the translation of this quote is no doubt highly Anglicized, the gist of it seems to be Hopi.

12. Adams and Hull 1980, pp. 20–27.

13. Miller 1910, p. 4.

14. Adams and Hull 1980, p. 22.

15. Bourke 1984, pp. 25 and 115; Donaldson 1893, p. 46; Means 1960, p. 53.

16. Nequatewa 1967, pp. 50–51; Courlander 1971, p. 31; Voth 1905b, p. 25; Emory Sekaquaptewa, personal communication, 1983.

17. H. James 1974, pp. 107–16.

18. Ibid., pp. 100–101. See also E. Sekaquaptewa 1972, pp. 253–54.

19. Courlander 1982, pp. 144–45; H. James 1974, p. 101; Yava 1978, p. 120.

20. Kabotie 1977, pp. 59–60.

21. Titiev 1944a, pp. 72–73.

22. Donaldson 1893, p. 56.

23. Titiev 1944a, pp. 73–74.

24. Crane 1926, p. 167; Voth 1905b, p. 21.

25. F. Hodge et al. 1922, pp. 258, 259, 263, 264, and 266.

26. Ibid., p. 274.

27. H. James 1974, pp. 117–20.

28. Ibid., p. 284; Dorsey and Voth 1901, p. 9.

29. H. James 1974, pp. 112–16.

30. Dorsey and Voth 1901, p. 10; Titiev 1944a, p. 80.

31. See U.S. District Court 1962.

32. Hack 1942a.

33. Titiev 1944a, pp. 73–74.

34. F. Hodge et al. 1922, p. 264. Spider clan members may have accepted the idea that they originated death in order to facilitate the Oraibi split.

35. Voth 1905b, p. 12.

36. Courlander 1971, pp. 31–32; Clemmer 1978, p. 47.

37. Maasaw is clearly ancestor to the Fire clan, but many Hopi myths state that the Fire clan refused to lead in the beginning when asked. See Courlander 1971, p. 32, and Yava 1978, p. 49. Titiev 1944a, pp. 155–56,

related an oral tradition in which the Fire clan explicitly names Maasaw as clan ancestor.

38. H. James 1974, p. 135; Titiev 1944a, p. 82; Talayesva 1942, p. 109.

39. E. Sekaquaptewa 1972, p. 249; Kabotie 1977, p. 4. The Hopi Milo Kalectaca translates Hotevilla as "to skin off one's back," a common misconception among Hopis not from Third Mesa; see Kalectaca 1978, p. 176. Courlander 1982, p. 245, was given two meanings for Hotevilla by Hopi informants: "cedar slope" and "scrape back."

40. E. Sekaquaptewa 1972, p. 247.

41. See Whiteley 1988a.

42. E. Sekaquaptewa 1972, p. 247.

43. The profaning of Hopi ceremonies may have been the biggest reason for the split; Whiteley was told that the main reason was to end the ceremonial cycle.

44. Bennett 1936, p. 372.

45. Talayesva 1942, p. 88; Qoyawayma 1964, p. 30.

46. That both Hopi factions ultimately wanted to resist oppression and acculturation by white Americans is hinted at by several government employees, who sensed that the friendlies cooperated with the superordinate society in order to better preserve their own autonomy. See Whiteley 1983, pp. 41–44.

47. Courlander 1982, pp. 126–27; Qoyawayma 1964, pp. 47–48; E. Sekaquaptewa 1972, p. 248; Talayesva 1942, pp. 109–10; Titiev 1944a, pp. 74 and 86.

48. E. Sekaquaptewa 1972, p. 249, stated that only Yukioma was aware of the reasons for migrating to Hotevilla rather than to Kawestima, but Nequatewa 1967, p. 132 n. 47, thought the reason was fear of Navajos.

49. Crane 1926, p. 188.

50. H. James 1974, pp. 134 and 143; Talayesva 1942, p. 243; Titiev 1944a, p. 95.

51. Titiev 1944a, p. 85. E. Sekaquaptewa 1962, p. 252, noted that even though Lololoma chose Tawaquaptewa as his successor, he denied him full title by not having the One Horn priests ordain him by washing his hair.

52. Whiteley 1982, pp. 498–99.

53. Lololoma earlier had sent some Hopi families to farm at Moencopi, too; see Nagata 1970, pp. 37–38.

54. Some Hopis also say that Tawaquaptewa was buried with his *mong-koho* (chief's stick), which signified that he desired no successor as village chief. It is important to remember, though, that Tawaquaptewa never went through the hairwashing rite that ordains a village chief and may never have possessed the right to discontinue either the ceremonial cycle or the office of village chief.

55. Titiev 1944a, p. 95. For a fuller version of this prophecy, see Whiteley 1982, p. 500. After the Hopi lose everything they have, this prophecy states, they will crawl back to Oraibi on hands and knees and the ceremonies will be restored.

56. Kabotie 1977, pp. 29 and 38. Don Talayesva also went through a

period of time wishing he were white, and this theme runs through Polingaysi Qoyawayma's autobiography; see Talayesva 1942, pp. 114–19, and Qoyawayma 1964.

57. Fear 1981.
58. H. James 1974, pp. 123–29.
59. Stephen 1936, p. 780.
60. Qoyawayma 1964, pp. 93–94.
61. H. James 1974, pp. 162–75.
62. Crane n.d.
63. H. James 1974, p. 185.
64. Ibid., pp. 190–91.
65. For a detailed discussion of the Hopi response to the Indian Reorganization Act, see Clemmer 1986.
66. A number of problems between the village chief and the Tribal Council on First Mesa have been reported in the 1980s. See *Qua'Töqti,* Sept. 15, 1983, p. 1; Jan. 6, 1984, p. 1; Jan. 26, 1984, p. 1; Feb. 2, 1984, pp. 1, 6.
67. Terrance Honvantewa, Second Mesa, personal communication, 1980; *Qua'Töqti,* Oct. 28, 1982, p. 5.
68. *Qua'Töqti,* Sept. 23, 1982, p. 4.
69. Nagata 1970, p. 93.
70. See Robert F. Berkhofer, Jr., *The White Man's Indian: Images of the American Indian from Columbus to the Present,* New York: Knopf, 1978, for a discussion of the way many Native Americans accept the stereotypes of their conquerors. Courlander 1982, p. xv n. 9, was told by a Hopi that he must choose to talk with either the progressives or the traditionalists: "If you are going to the progressives for help . . . then I can't do anything for you."

Five. Compartmentalization and Prophecy

1. *Qua'Töqti,* Sept. 2, 1982, p. 2; Oct. 6, 1983, p. 2; Oct. 20, 1983, p. 2.
2. E. Sekaquaptewa 1976, p. 40; Spicer 1971. For another Hopi understanding of the way a Hopi can live in two worlds, see Sekakuku 1939, p. 16. Compartmentalization is an interesting theory but seems problematic when applied to the contemporary Western religious environment. For instance, Buber 1970, p. 99, argued that the religious life cannot remain alive if human existence is divided into independent realms such as economic and religious. Buber, however, was speaking to a dominant culture that had the power to chart its own destiny to a degree. I am not certain that he would have argued the same for an oppressed people, since oppressed peoples are pulled into the dominant culture of competition and greed against their will.
3. For example, Abbot Sekaquaptewa stated that Hopi participation in formal education and federal government support programs should be perceived as means to an end rather than ends in themselves; *Qua'Töqti,* Oct. 25, 1984, p. 2; Nov. 15, 1984, p. 2. For Emory Sekaquaptewa's view of legal training among the Hopi, see Shorris 1971, pp. 127–29.

4. H. Sekaquaptewa 1969, p. 248. E. Sekaquaptewa 1980b, p. 7, related this prophecy about education: "In our youth, old men of the day reiterated the teaching of prophecy that a day will come to pass when new generations of Hopi will become as the ears and tongues for the old. We understood this to mean education in the ways of the white man in his schools so that we may help our people find a smoother path in the world dominated by the white man."

5. *Qua'Töqti,* Oct. 11, 1984, p. 2.

6. E. Sekaquaptewa 1972, p. 260.

7. See *Qua'Töqti,* Sept. 1, 1983, p. 4.

8. See, for example, ibid., Sept. 9, 1982, p. 2.

9. Ibid., Sept. 23, 1982, p. 3.

10. Ibid., Dec. 8, 1983, p. 3. Hopi traditionalists and progressives are divided over the Big Mountain controversy. Navajos have been ordered by the federal government to leave the Big Mountain area because the land belongs to the Hopi. Hopi traditionalists seem to think that Hopis and Navajos can share the land in a friendly way—a position most Hopis resist, given the long history of Navajo skirmishes with the Hopi and encroachment on Hopi lands.

11. Page 1982a, p. 216. For a brief history of the Hopi aboriginal land claim, see *To Provide the Exchange of Certain Lands between the Hopi and Navajo Indian Tribes,* Hearings on H.R. 4281 before the Committee on Interior and Insular Affairs, 99th Congress, 2d Session, 288–301 (1986).

12. I am referring to the many Navajos who live on traditional Hopi lands outside the Big Mountain area, where relocation of Navajos has begun.

13. Kennard 1965, p. 27.

14. Ibid., p. 25.

15. Ibid., p. 27.

16. Ibid., pp. 27–28.

17. *Qua'Töqti,* June 30, 1983, p. 1.

18. Ibid., Mar. 10, 1983, p. 2.

19. Ibid., Oct. 27, 1984, p. 4.

20. Kennard 1965, p. 29.

21. Ibid.

22. "Hopi Tribe Clings to Peace Beneath the Gaze of Gods," *Arizona Republic,* July 20, 1980, sec. A, p. 10.

23. Whiteley 1982, chap. 6.

24. Hait 1980, p. 25. Abbot Sekaquaptewa wrote (*Qua'Töqti,* Jan. 28, 1983, p. 2) that wage earning among the Hopi has resulted in less and less farming by the Hopi over the past forty years but not in its complete abandonment by most families. Furthermore, he stated that even when wage earning draws people away from farming, "the importance of the land and its increase remains strong in the hearts of the Hopi people."

25. Whiteley 1982, p. 311.

26. See comments by Radford Quamahongnewa and Emory Sekaquaptewa in *Katsi: Happiness, Health and Peace* 1984, pp. 19–27 and 46–50.

27. Ibid., pp. 46–50.

28. E. Sekaquaptewa 1972, p. 253.

29. Talayesva 1942, p. 380.

30. For maps showing the history of Hopi Reservation, see E. Sekaquaptewa 1972, p. 260; Page 1982a, p. 610; and *Hopi Tutu-veh-ni* 1986, pp. 8–9.

31. See Page 1982a, p. 611.

32. The controversial Big Mountain land dispute has spawned several federal statutes and a multitude of case decisions. Because the issue is so emotionally charged and widely misunderstood, I have chosen not to discuss it at length in this book.

33. The Hopi lost their legal battle to prevent further development of Snow Bowl in both the district and the appellate court. In the trial Abbot Sekaquaptewa testified on behalf of the Hopi: "It is my opinion that in the long run if the expansion is permitted, we will not be able successfully to teach our people that it is a sacred place. If the ski resort remains or is expanded, our people will not accept the view that this is the sacred Home of the Kachinas." See *Wilson v. Block*, 708 F. 2d 735, 740 (D.C. Cir. 1984), *cert. denied*, 464 U.S. 956 (1984).

34. I have heard many Hopi people complain that cooperation with the federal government has only resulted in the further domination of the Hopi. Also see *Qua'Töqti*, Sept. 30, 1982; Oct. 17, 1982; Dec. 16, 1982; Mar. 17, 1983; Mar. 24, 1983; Apr. 28, 1983; May 26, 1983; June 9, 1983; and June 16, 1983.

35. Ibid., Apr. 19, 1984, p. 2.

36. Ibid., Apr. 21, 1983, p. 1; May 5, 1983, p. 1; May 12, 1983, p. 2; May 19, 1983, p. 2.

37. Ibid., July 7, 1983, pp. 1, 2; July 6, 1984, p. 1.

38. *Enforcement of the Indian Civil Rights Act*, p. 118.

39. This discussion is taken, except where otherwise noted, from H. James 1974, pp. 215–22.

40. Hack 1942b.

41. Page 1982b, p. 151.

42. Eliade 1978, p. 53.

43. Mischa Titiev, "A Hopi Salt Expedition," *American Anthropologist* 39 (1973): 245.

44. Talayesva 1942, p. 242.

45. Beaglehole 1937, p. 57.

46. Wilson 1980, p. 38.

47. Kabotie 1977, p. 136.

48. Page 1982b, pp. 192–93.

49. Clemmer 1970. See the letter (p. 19) written by several Hopis in 1970 to the Tribal Council imploring the council not to sign a coal mining lease with Peabody. The authors stated that "our religion and way of life says that water is the most important thing for life. . . . A train or a truck can carry coal, but only the water can make our crops grow and put fluid in our bodies."

50. See Capps 1976, p. 112.

51. *Qua'Töqti*, Aug. 19, 1982; Nov. 4, 1982.

52. Ibid., Feb. 10, 1983, p. 2; Jan. 6, 1984, p. 2.
53. Ibid., Apr. 28, 1983; Aug. 25, 1983; Sept. 15, 1983, p. 1; Oct. 20, 1983, p. 1; Oct. 27, 1983, p. 1; Nov. 10, 1983, p. 1; Dec. 8, 1983, p. 1.
54. Ibid., Nov. 18, 1982, p. 1; Dec. 2, 1982, p. 2; Jan. 28, 1983, p. 1; Sept. 1, 1983, p. 4; Feb. 16, 1984, p. 1; Feb. 23, 1984, p. 1. See Indian Self-Determination and Education Assistance Act of 1975, Pub. L. no. 93–638, 88 Stat. 2203 (codified at 25 U.S.C. sections 450–450n, 455–458e) (1982).
55. Qua'Töqti, Nov. 15, 1984, p. 2.
56. Ibid., Oct. 27, 1983, p. 1.
57. Emory Sekaquaptewa, personal communication, Tucson, 1984; Qua'Töqti, Jan. 12, 1984, p. 2.
58. Fred Kabotie, Hopi Symposium, Third Mesa, 1981. Similarly, Radford Quamohongnewa lamented that novices at an initiation rite at Shongopavi had to be instructed in English because they did not understand Hopi; Katsi: Happiness, Health and Peace 1984, p. 47.
59. Emory Sekaquaptewa, personal communication, Third Mesa, 1983; Fred Eggan, Santa Fe, N.M., 1983.
60. Qua'Töqti, Nov. 3, 1983, p. 2.
61. Kabotie 1977, pp. 106–7.
62. Courlander 1982, pp. xxvii–xxix; Qua'Töqti, June 29, 1984, pp. 1 and 5.
63. Cox 1970, p. 91.
64. Qua'Töqti, Mar. 10, 1983, p. 2. Nonetheless, the work week disrupts the Hopi ceremonial calendar, a point Radford Quamahongnewa made in Katsi: Happiness, Health and Peace 1984, p. 49.
65. Quoted in Athia Hardt, "Urban Hopi Indians Feel Torn between 2 Worlds," unpublished article in possession of John D. Loftin.
66. Kabotie 1977, pp. 77–95 and 113–28.
67. Qua'Töqti, Mar. 10, 1983, p. 1; Mar. 31, 1983, p. 1.
68. Kabotie 1977, p. 134; Artist Hopid, Profile Artist Hopid.
69. Younger and Masayesva 1983, p. 11.
70. Wright 1973, p. 37, and 1977, pp. 78 and 79; Malotki 1983a, pp. 36–37.
71. Qua'Töqti, July 20, 1984, p. 3. Two Hopi elders wrote that the ceremony was performed according to traditional custom and that the children were quiet and respectful.
72. Anonymous, personal communication, 1980; Titiev 1944a, p. 106.
73. Talayesva 1942, p. 380.
74. Honheptewa 1988, p. x.
75. Yava 1978, p. 78.
76. Qua'Töqti, Mar. 15, 1984, p. 1.
77. Ibid., July 21, 1983, p. 2.
78. Ibid., May 19, 1983, p. 1; May 26, 1983, p. 1; Apr. 19, 1984, p. 1. See also Elaine Shannon, "Lost Idols of Shungopavi," Newsweek, July 31, 1983, pp. 32–33.
79. Page 1983.
80. Ibid., p. 61.
81. Qua'Töqti, Oct. 11, 1983, p. 1; Feb. 23, 1984, p. 2.

82. Ibid., June 16, 1983, pp. 1 and 4; Apr. 16, 1984, p. 2; Oct. 20, 1983, p. 2.

83. Yava 1978, p. 36; Courlander 1982, p. 27.

84. For a discussion of the relation between meaning and modes of manifestation, see Long 1963a, p. 25.

85. *Qua'Töqti,* June 7, 1984, pp. 1 and 4; June 15, 1984, p. 1; June 21, 1984, p. 2.

86. See, for example, *Qua'Töqti,* Oct. 20, 1983, p. 2; Courlander 1982, p. 130. I should note, with regard to this last reference, that Homer Cooyama, who blamed whites for the loss of Hopi traditions, was himself a Christian.

87. Yava 1978, pp. 133 and 136. Of course, one must keep in mind that Yava is also a Tewa; the Tewa are sometimes critical of their Hopi neighbors.

88. Talayesva 1942, p. 336.

89. *Qua'Töqti,* Aug. 4, 1983, p. 2. See also Radford Quamahongnewa's comments about laziness in *Katsi: Happiness, Health and Peace* 1984, p. 49.

90. *Qua'Töqti,* Jan. 26, 1984, p. 5.

91. Ibid., Oct. 7, 1983, p. 4. See also the self-critical statements by Kahsa (Qasa) in ibid., Jan. 12, 1984, p. 6.

92. Ibid., Sept. 16, 1982, p. 2.

93. Ibid., Dec. 2, 1982, p. 2; Dec. 9, 1982, p. 2.

94. Ibid., Mar. 1, 1984, p. 2.

95. Ibid., Mar. 10, 1983, p. 2.

96. Ibid., Apr. 19, 1984, p. 5; Mar. 29, 1984, p. 2. It is not clear that the addition of Santa Claus and Kachina dances on Mother's Day is necessarily bad, but it is reported negatively by many of my Hopi consultants.

97. Talayesva 1942, p. 224. This lamentation of loss of Hopi spirituality is often heard today among Hopis. See also *Qua'Töqti,* Dec. 30, 1982, p. 2; July 28, 1983, p. 2.

98. *Qua'Töqti,* Aug. 11, 1983, p. 2.

99. Ibid., Oct. 27, 1983, p. 2.

100. Ibid., Mar. 8, 1984, p. 2.

101. Ibid., Oct. 25, 1984, p. 2.

102. Ibid., Nov. 10, 1983, p. 1; Jan. 26, 1984, pp. 1 and 6; Mar. 15, 1984, p. 4; Nov. 8, 1984, p. 1.

103. Ibid., Sept. 15, 1983, p. 5; Feb. 8, 1984, p. 4.

104. Ibid., Jan. 19, 1984, p. 2.

105. Ibid., Mar. 15, 1984, p. 1.

106. Ibid., Mar. 22, 1984, p. 1.

Six. Sacred and Human

1. *Qua'Töqti,* Sept. 1, 1983, p. 2.
2. Courlander 1982, p. 245.
3. Shorris 1971, pp. 127 and 133. See also Malotki 1978, p. 203.
4. Emory Sekaquaptewa, personal communication, 1980.

5. Hopi Symposium, Third Mesa, 1980. The remark was made by Abbot Sekaquaptewa, then tribal chairman.

6. *Qua'Töqti*, Nov. 11, 1982, p. 3.

7. H. James 1974, p. 222.

8. *Qua'Töqti*, Mar. 22, 1984, p. 3.

9. See *Qua'Töqti*, Nov. 3, 1983, p. 5.

10. Whorf 1950, p. 67.

11. C. F. Voegelin, F. M. Voeglin, and Laverne Masayesva Jeanne, "Hopi Semantics," in *Handbook of North American Indians*, vol. 9, Washington: Smithsonian, 1980, p. 582; Malotki 1983b, esp. the introduction and concluding remarks.

12. Whorf 1950, pp. 67–72. Bradfield 1973 echoed Whorf's view of Hopi time.

13. The Hopi are not philosophers in the formal sense and thus are not interested in the debates concerning free will and determinism in the West. Their view rejects formal logic in favor of a lived logic that seeks meaning in the world. Thus, if a Hopi says that all is predetermined so that he cannot help being *kahopi*, others will respond that Hopis have the spark of life and thus freedom to correct their behavior and thoughts. If, on the other hand, a Hopi states that he has freely brought destruction upon himself, others will say that such problems were determined from the beginning and thus are meaningful in the end. In all cases, life (and even death) is viewed as ultimately significant.

14. Quoted in C. Hodge 1980, p. 43.

15. *Qua'Töqti*, Nov. 3, 1983, p. 5.

16. Cushing 1923; Goldfrank 1948, pp. 244–50; Nequatewa 1967, pp. 50–51; Titiev 1944a, p. 71 n. 29; *Qua'Töqti*, Nov. 3, 1983, p. 5. In mythic terms, whether or not the myth of the elder white brother *(pahaana)* existed before the Hopi experience of white people is not pertinent, as I stated earlier. I have not thoroughly checked the Spanish documents about the existence of the myth during Spanish-Hopi contacts, but it is fair to say that the myth parallels Hopi-Mormon contact. See Peterson 1971.

17. Emory Sekaquaptewa, personal communication by letter, 1984.

18. Crane 1926, p. 167; Talayesva 1942, p. 420; Voth 1905b, p. 21; *Qua'Töqti*, Nov. 3, 1983, p. 5; Titiev 1944a, pp. 74–75.

19. Indeed, there is evidence that in 1905 Yukioma, the hostile leader at Oraibi, differentiated the true *pahaana* from the whites the Hopi had encountered. See Voth n.d.

20. Brandt 1954, esp. pp. 211–65. For contemporary Hopi remarks about the decline of traditional values, see *Qua'Töqti*, Aug. 12, 1982, p. 2; Sept. 2, 1982, p. 2; Sept. 9, 1982, p. 2.; Sept. 16, 1982, p. 2.

21. *Katsi: Happiness, Health and Peace* 1984, p. 19. See also *Qua'Töqti*, Aug. 4, 1983, p. 2.

22. Hardt, "Urban Hopi Indians Feel Torn Between 2 Worlds"; Hait 1980, p. 16.

23. *Qua'Töqti*, Oct. 11, 1984, p. 2.

24. Ibid., Aug. 7, 1980, p. 1.

25. Ibid., Mar. 3, 1983, p. 1.

26. H. James 1974, pp. 102–3; Page 1982b, pp. 216–17.

27. Hermenquaftewa 1971, p. 60.

28. Quoted in Page 1983, p. 62.

29. *Qua'Töqti*, Oct. 14, 1982, p. 6.

30. Ibid., Nov. 23, 1983, p. 1.

31. The Hopi Business Association, Tribal Employment Rights Office (TERO), Hopi Electronics Enterprise, Office of Business Enterprise Development (OBED), and Southwest Indian Development Enterprise (SIDE) promote Hopi economic self-sufficiency. See *Qua'Töqti*, July 21, 1983, pp. 1 and 7; Nov. 3, 1983, p. 1; Dec. 8, 1983, p. 1; Jan. 12, 1984, p. 5; Jan. 19, 1984, p. 1; Feb. 23, 1984, p. 1.

32. E. Sekaquaptewa 1976, p. 41.

33. See *Qua'Töqti*, Aug. 5, 1982, p. 2; Jan. 3, 1983, p. 2; July 14, 1983, p. 2.

34. See Capps 1976, p. 113.

35. *Qua'Töqti*, Apr. 5, 1984, p. 1.

36. In a sense, all factions and movements within Hopi, including Hopi traditionalists, must come to grips with American society and the U.S. government. Clemmer 1982 argued that traditionalists embody a contact strategy that contrasts with "cooperation with alien, dominant political authorities and which has come to be embodied and followed by the Hopi Tribal Council." Yet Clemmer himself noted that traditionalists seek aid from non-Hopi members of the dominant society. Therefore they too seek cooperation from the superordinate society, or at least from one of its factions.

37. Long 1985 argued that American religious studies should be discussed in terms of New World religions, since America is not simply European, Indian, or African; the religious orientations of many Americans, such as black Roman Catholics, he pointed out, do not fit into the traditional disciplinary categories of either America or religion.

Annotated Bibliography

Adams, E. Charles, and Deborah Hull. 1980. "The Prehistoric and Historic Occupation of the Hopi Mesas." In Washburn 1980. Good overview of Hopi prehistory and history.

Alvarado, Anita L. 1968. "Hopi Political Structure: A Response to a Marginal Agricultural Environment." *Southwestern Anthropological Association Newsletter* 10:7–13. Argues that the loosely organized political structure of the Hopi reveals the effect of a marginal, semidesert environment that precludes any significant agricultural surplus.

Artist Hopid. 1974. *Profile Artist Hopid.* Second Mesa, Ariz.: Hopi Arts and Crafts Guild. Description of the origin and purpose of the fine arts organization started after World War II by Fred Kabotie.

Beaglehole, Ernest. 1936. *Hopi Hunting and Hunting Ritual.* New Haven, Conn.: Yale University Press. Excellent account from Second Mesa.

———. 1937. *Notes on Hopi Economic Life.* New Haven, Conn.: Yale University Press. Fine description of many aspects of Hopi economic life, primarily from Second Mesa.

Beaglehole, Ernest, and Pearl Beaglehole. 1935. *Hopi of the Second Mesa.* Menasha, Wis.: American Anthropological Association. Good description of Hopi sorcery, burial practices, dream interpretation, warfare, and personal matters from sexual intercourse to childrearing practices.

Bennett, John W. 1936. "The Interpretation of Pueblo Culture: A Question of Values." *Southwestern Journal of Anthropology* 2:361–74. Argues from Hopi and Zuni materials that the scholarly dispute over whether Pueblo society is organic and harmonious or divisive and repressive can be better understood in terms of a means-end paradigm: the Pueblos are somewhat divisive so that they can survive as peoples.

Black, Mary E. 1984. "Maidens and Mothers: An Analysis of Hopi Corn Metaphors." *Ethnology* 23:279–88. Demonstrates the centrality of the corn metaphor among the Hopi based on an analysis of the Hopi language.

Black, Robert A. 1965. "A Content Analysis of 81 Hopi Indian Chants." Ph.D. diss., Indiana University. Thorough listing (in Hopi and English) and linguistic analysis of three types of Hopi chants: work activities, social activities, grievances.

Boas, Franz. 1948. *Race, Language and Culture.* New York: Macmillan.

Classifies Native Americans by physiology, language, and way of life.

Bordieu, Pierre. 1977. *Outline of a Theory of Practice*. Trans. Richard Nice. Cambridge: Cambridge University Press. Attempts to overcome the problem of theory and practice by arguing that theory always inhabits practice; examples from the Algerian Kabyle.

Bourke, John G. 1984. *The Snake Dance of the Moquis of Arizona*. Tucson: University of Arizona Press. Especially valuable in relating details of Hopi material life in the late nineteenth century. Foreword by Emory Sekaquaptewa.

Bradfield, R. Maitland. 1971. "The Changing Pattern of Hopi Agriculture." Royal Anthropological Institute Occasional Paper, no. 30. London. Done in conjunction with the Hopi Harry Masai'yamtiwa; demonstrates the ecological viability of Hopi agricultural techniques as well as some recent changes in farming practices due to ecological change.

———. 1973. *A Natural History of Associations: A Study in the Meaning of Community*. Vol. 2. London: Duckworth. One of the most thorough syntheses of data about the Hopi since Titiev's *Old Oraibi;* widely accepted for its theoretical insights. However, it is religiously problematical because it fractures the unity of theory and practice, ignores sacred time, and argues that mimetic magic was the earliest form of prayer.

Brandt, Richard B. 1954. *Hopi Ethics: A Theoretical Analysis*. Chicago: University of Chicago Press. Contains numerous Hopi responses to ethical questions and explores the decline of traditional Hopi values from 1946 to 1948.

Breunig, Robert, and Michael Lomatuway'ma. 1983. "Hopi: Scenes of Everyday Life." *Plateau* 55:1–32. Pictorial overview of Hopi life in the early twentieth century; photographs by Emry Kopta.

Brown, Joseph Epes. 1976. "The Roots of Renewal." In Capps 1976, pp. 25–34. Laments the loss of spiritual roots by Western civilization but hopes its spirituality can be renewed through understanding Native Americans.

Buber, Martin. 1970. *I and Thou*. Trans. Walter Kaufman. New York: Scribner. Discussion of the human experience of the sacred as distant yet related, transcendent yet immanent.

Buckley, Thomas. 1982. "Menstruation and the Power of Yoruk Women: Methods in Cultural Reconstruction." *American Ethnologist* 9:47–60. Discusses female religious symbolism.

———. 1989. "The Goddess That Stepped Forth from the Word." *History of Religions* 28:357–59. Critical review of Gill's *Mother Earth;* asserts the centrality of earth as a metaphor for Native American religious consciousness.

Capps, Walter H., ed. 1976. *Seeing with a Native Eye: Essays on Native American Religion*. New York: Harper & Row. A fine collection of short papers on Native American religion by Åke Hultkrantz, Joseph Brown, Sam Gill, Emory Sekaquaptewa, Barre Toelken,

Scott Momaday, and Richard Comstock. Includes a panel discussion held at the University of California at Santa Barbara in which Emory Sekaquaptewa talked about problems in researching Native American religions.

Clemmer, Richard O. 1970. "Economic Development vs. Aboriginal Land Use: An Attempt to Predict Culture Change on an Indian Reservation in Arizona." Unpublished manuscript. Documents the manipulation of Hopis by the Interior Department in urging them to sell coal rights to private businesses and presents data on groundwater loss and air pollution resulting from coal mining and burning in and around Hopi.

————. 1978. *Continuities of Hopi Culture Change*. Ramona, Calif.: Acoma Books. Collection of twentieth-century Hopi oral traditions from Hopi traditionalists. Includes some inaccurate statements—see 1982 critical review by Emory Sekaquaptewa, *Ethnohistory* 19:73–74.

————. 1982. "The Rise of the Traditionalists and the New Politics." Unpublished manuscript. Relates the Hopi traditionalist movement to various anthropological theories concerning responses to dominance.

————. 1986. "Hopis, Western Shoshones, and Southern Utes: Three Different Responses to the Indian Reorganization Act of 1934." *American Indian Culture and Research Journal* 10:15–40. Detailed case study; asks important questions about the appropriateness of the Indian Reorganization Act in affecting Hopi political values.

Corres, Elliot. 1900. *On the Trail of a Spanish Pioneer*. New York: Harper & Row. Hopi life as seen by an early Spanish explorer of the Southwest.

Courlander, Harold. 1971. *The Fourth World of the Hopis*. New York: Crown. Hopi myths retold. Courlander used consultants from all three mesas and briefly analyzes their different mythologies.

————. 1982. *Hopi Voices: Recollections, Traditions, and Narratives of the Hopi Indians*. Albuquerque: University of New Mexico Press. Hopi myths and traditions collected directly from Hopi consultants in English; lists name and village affiliation of each informant but does not distinguish between remarks of an uninitiated, Christian Hopi, for example, and those of a fully initiated clan elder.

Cox, Bruce A. 1970. "What Is Hopi Gossip About? Information Management and Hopi Factions." *Man* 5:88–98. Argues that Hopi factions use gossip to stigmatize their adversaries in order to gain public approval for their own group.

Crane, Leo. 1926. *Indians of the Enchanted Desert*. Boston: Little, Brown.

————, ed. N.d. "History of the Moqui Indian Reservation, Compiled from Annual Reports of Indian Agents at Keams Canyon and Fort Defiance." Manuscript 135-2-3 of the Museum of Northern Arizona, Flagstaff. Important historical data on early Hopi–U.S. troubles and disputes.

Curtis, Edward S. 1970. *The North American Indian*. Vol. 12. New York:

Johnson Reprint. Originally published by Harvard University Press, 1922. Drawn from investigations primarily at Walpi, First Mesa. Includes numerous photographs; a good overview of Hopi life, clan histories, and myths; and a brief glossary.

Cushing, Frank H. 1923. "Origin Myth from Oraibi." *Journal of American Folk-Lore* 25:163–70. One of the oldest versions of the Hopi emergence myth in print; recorded in 1883 and later edited by Elsie Clews Parsons.

Dardel, Eric. 1954. "The Mythic, according to the Ethnological Work of Maurice Leenhardt." *Diogenes*, no. 7, 33–51.

Deloria, Vine. 1970. *We Talk, You Listen.* New York: Delta. Deloria, a Sioux, has written extensively on white–Native American cultural contact and relations.

———. *God Is Red.* 1973. New York: Grosset & Dunlap.

Donaldson, Thomas. 1893. *Moqui Pueblo Indians of Arizona and Pueblo Indians of New Mexico: Extra Census Bulletin.* Washington: U.S. Census Printing Office. Describes housing, clothing, and other aspects of Hopi material life at the end of the nineteenth century.

Dorsey, George A., and Henry R. Voth. 1901. *The Oraibi Soyal Ceremony.* Chicago: Field Columbian Museum.

———. 1902. *The Mishongnovi Ceremonies of the Snake and Antelope Fraternities.* Chicago: Field Columbian Museum. These two works outline Hopi ceremonies in detail.

Dozier, Edward P. 1970. *The Pueblo Indians of North America.* New York: Holt, Rinehart & Winston. Important work by a fine anthropologist who was also a Pueblo Indian.

———. 1971. "Rio Grande Pueblos." In Spicer 1971, pp. 94–186. Traces history and character of Rio Grande Pueblo–European cultural contact, interpreting Pueblo responses as "compartmentalization," a process by which the Pueblos participated superficially in the superordinate society while remaining firmly attached to aboriginal values and, when possible, practices.

Durkheim, Emile, and Marcel Mauss. 1963. *Primitive Classification.* Trans. R. Needham. Chicago: University of Chicago Press. Classic social structural work attempts to demonstrate that the classification of nature by "primitive" peoples facilitates social integration.

Earle, Edwin, and Edward A. Kennard. 1971. *Hopi Kachinas.* 2d ed. New York: Museum of the American Indian, Heye Foundation. Excellent introduction to Hopi kachinas with important theoretical insights by Kennard, who as a graduate student from the University of Chicago followed Leslie White into Hopi in 1931.

Eggan, Dorothy. 1948. "The General Problem of Hopi Adjustment." In *Personality in Nature, Society and Culture,* ed. C. Kluckhohn and H. A. Murray. New York: Knopf.

———. 1949. "The Significance of Dreams for Anthropological Research." *American Anthropologist* 51:177–98.

———. 1952. "The Manifest Content of Dreams: A Challenge to Social

Science." *American Anthropologist* 54:465–89. A psychological perspective on Hopi dream life; important for religious studies because the Hopi experience dreams as religiously significant.

Eggan, Fred R. 1933. "The Kinship System and Social Organization of the Western Pueblos with Special References to the Hopi Indians." Ph.D. diss., University of Chicago.

———. 1950. *Social Organization of the Western Pueblos*. Chicago: University of Chicago Press. Keen insights on Pueblo social structure by a scholar who like Kennard followed Leslie White into Hopi as a graduate student in 1931.

Eliade, Mircea. 1954. *The Myth of the Eternal Return or, Cosmos and History.* Trans. Willard R. Trask. Princeton, N.J.: Princeton University Press. Eliade's well-known works cover many dimensions of the history of religions.

———. 1958. *Patterns in Comparative Religion*. Trans. Rosemary Sheed. New York: Sheed & Ward.

———. 1969. *The Quest: History and Meaning in Religions*. Chicago: University of Chicago Press.

———. 1978. *A History of Religious Ideas*. Vol. 1. Trans. Willard R. Trask. Chicago: University of Chicago Press.

Elkin, A. P., Catherine Berndt, and Ronald Berndt. 1950. *Art in Arnhem Land*. Chicago: University of Chicago Press. Emphasizes the religous dimensions of art by Australian aborigines.

Enforcement of the Indian Civil Rights Act. Hearing before the United States Commission on Civil Rights, July 20, 1988. Statements by Hopi Tribal Chairman Ivan Sidney, Vice Chairman Vernon Masayesva, and Tribal Court Counsel Frances Jue.

Fear, Jacqueline, 1981. "Assimilation and the School: Dichotomization of Indian and White Society." In *North American Indian Studies: European Contribution*, pp. 129–44. Gottingen: Edition Herodot. Historical overview of how the U.S. attempted to "convert" and "civilize" Native Americans through formal education.

Fewkes, J. Walter. 1895. "The Tusayan New Fire Ceremony." *Proceedings of the Boston Society of Natural History* 26:422–58.

———. 1900a. "The New Fire Ceremony at Walpi." *American Anthropologist* 2:80–138. Straightforward description of First Mesa Wuwtsim ceremonies by the most prolific author on the Hopi. Fewkes wrote nearly one hundred works dealing with almost every aspect of Hopi life.

———. 1900b. "Tusayan Migration Traditions." Smithsonian Institution, Bureau of American Ethnology, 19th Annual Report for 1897–98, pt. 2, pp. 573–633. Washington: Government Printing Office. Excellent collection of migration myths, especially from First Mesa, though Fewkes mistakenly assumed that these myths were historically accurate and does not concentrate on their religious significance.

Fewkes, J. W., and A. M. Stephen. 1892. "The Na-ac-nai-ya: A Tusayan Initiation Ceremony." *Journal of American Folk-Lore* 5:189–221. Description of a First Mesa Wuwtsim initiation by two long-time visitors to Hopi.

————. 1893. "The Pa-lu-lu-kon-ti: A Tusayan Ceremony." *Journal of American Folk-Lore* 6:269–94. Detailed description from First Mesa of the Water Serpent dance.

Fickeler, Paul. 1962. "Fundamental Questions in the Geography of Religions." In *Readings in Cultural Geography*, ed. and trans. P. L. Wagner and M. W. Mikesell, pp. 94–117. Chicago: University of Chicago Press. Argues that the geographer of religion should examine how religion affects landscape, demography, and environment.

Fletcher, A. O. 1910. "Wakonda: Handbook of American Indians." *Bureau of American Ethnology Bulletin* 30:897–98. Discussion of the sacred among the Omaha, Osage, and Ponca.

Forde, C. Daryll. 1931. "Hopi Agriculture and Land Ownership." *Journal of the Royal Anthropological Institute* 61:357–405.

————. 1934. *Habitat, Economy and Society: A Geographical Introduction to Ethnology.* London: Methuen. Shows how the Hopi way paralleled the desert environment.

Geertz, Armin W. 1982. "The Sa'lakwmanawyat Sacred Puppet Ceremonial among the Hopi Indians of Arizona: A Preliminary Investigation." *Anthropos* 77:163–90. Carefully written, well-researched account of a little-known aspect of Hopi ceremonialism by a historian of religions.

Geertz, Armin W., and Michael Lomatuway'ma. 1987. *Children of Cottonwood: Piety and Ceremonialism in Hopi Indian Puppetry.* Lincoln: University of Nebraska Press. An extensive work on Hopi puppetry that includes a large number of bilingual texts with important commentaries. Concentrates on language study.

Gill, Sam D. 1976. "The Shadow of a Vision Yonder." In Capps 1976, pp. 51–55. Discusses briefly the symbolism embodied in the Hopi kachina initiation.

————. 1977. "Hopi Kachina Cult Initiation: The Shocking Beginning to the Hopis' Religious Life." *Journal of the American Academy of Religion* 45(suppl.):447–514. Detailed treatment of the Hopi kachina initiation and the way in which it introduces Hopi neophytes to adult religious life.

————. 1977–78. "Prayer as Person: The Performative Force in Navajo Prayer Acts." *History of Religions* 17:143–57. Criticizes the view that Navajo prayer is compulsive magic.

————. 1981. *Sacred Words: A Study of Navajo Religion and Prayer.* Westport, Conn.: Greenwood. A critique of Gladys Reichard's *Navajo Indian Religion*, which argues that Navajo prayer rites are magical.

————. 1982. *Native American Religions: An Introduction.* Belmont, Calif.: Wadsworth. Thematic overview; has some information on the Hopi.

————. 1987. *Mother Earth: An American Story.* Chicago: University of Chicago Press. Argues that the Native American symbol Mother

Earth did not become important until the late nineteenth and twentieth centuries.

Goldfrank, Esther S. 1948. "The Impact of Situation and Personality on Four Hopi Emergence Myths." *Southwestern Journal of Anthropology* 4:241–61. Attempts to demonstrate that Hopi mythology cannot be understood apart from the historical circumstances, mood, and clan of the informant.

Gross, Rita M. 1980. "Menstruation and Childbirth as Ritual and Religious Experience among Native Australians." In *Unspoken Worlds: Women's Religious Lives in Non-Western Cultures*, ed. Nancy A. Falk and Rita M. Gross, pp. 277–92. San Francisco: Harper & Row. Demonstrates the almost mute mode through which female Australian aborigines experience the sacred.

Hack, John T. 1942a. *The Changing Physical Environment of the Hopi Indians of Arizona*. Cambridge, Mass.: Peabody Museum. Traces environmental changes since the late Paleolithic.

———. 1942b. *Prehistoric Coal Mining in the Jeddito Valley, Arizona*. Cambridge, Mass.: Peabody Museum, 1942. Reconstruction of Hopi prehistoric coal mining based on archaeological finds.

Hait, Pam. 1980. "On Being Hopi: A Personal View." *Arizona Highways* 56:16–28. Expresses a number of Hopi views.

Hargrave, Lyndon L. 1939. "Bird Bones from Abandoned Indian Dwellings in Arizona and Utah." *Condor* 41:206–10. Suggests that parrots may once have been indigenous to the San Francisco Peaks.

Hermenquaftewa, Andrew. 1971. "The Hopi Way of Life Is the Way of Peace." In *Red Power: The American Indians' Fight for Freedom*, ed. Alvin Josephy. New York: American Heritage Press. The myth of Hopi origins told by a traditionalist Hopi Bluebird chief from Shungopavi, who also relates a few basic points about Hopi religion and makes a plea that the Hopi may live in peace.

Hewitt, J. N. B. 1901. "Orenda and a Definition of Religion." *American Anthropologist* OS 4:33–46. An Iroquois discusses the Iroquois term for an impersonal supernatural power, *orenda*.

Hieb, Louis A. 1972. "The Hopi Ritual Clown: Life as It Should Not Be." Ph.D. diss., Princeton University. A large collection of descriptions and interpretations of Hopi clown rituals, preceded by an overview of Hopi religion.

———. 1979a. "Hopi World View." In Alfonso Ortiz, ed., *Handbook of North American Indians*, vol. 9, pp. 577–80. Washington: Smithsonian. Succinct overview of the Hopi understanding of time and space.

———. 1979b. "Masks and Meaning: A Contextual Approach to the Hopi *Tüvi'kü*." In *University of Northern Colorado Museum of Anthropology Occasional Publications*, no. 33, pp. 62–79. Greeley, Colo. Discusses Hopi religion through an interpretation of the Hopi Malo kachina; shows that the "spiritual substance" that is ultimate reality is a basic structure of Hopi kinship.

Hillerman, Tony. 1980. "The Hopi Migrations: Journey to the Center of the

Universe." *Arizona Highways* 56:9–15. Contains important comments of Hopis George Nasoftie, Taylor Wazri, and Stanley Honanie.

Hodge, Carl. 1980. "The Hopi Prophecies: A Vast and Complex Liturgy." *Arizona Highways* 56:43–44. Contains important comments of Hopis Starlie Lomayaktewa, Percy Lomahquahu, Abbot Sekaquaptewa, and George Nasoftie.

Hodge, Frederick W., et al. 1922. "Contributions to Hopi History." *American Anthropologist* 24:253–98. Brief introduction by Hodge plus articles by Frank Cushing, J. Walter Fewkes, and Elsie Clews Parsons with emphasis on Oraibi in 1882, 1890, and 1920; Parsons also writes about Shungopavi (Shohau'pavi) in 1920.

Honheptewa, Leigh Jenkins. 1988. Forword. In Whiteley 1988, pp. ix–x. States that Bacavi residents continue "the true Hopi spirit of cooperation, humility, and thoughtful prayers" even though the ceremonial calendar was "laid to rest."

Hopi: Songs of the Fourth World. 1984. New Day Films, 22 Riverview Drive, Wayne, N.J. 07470. 58 minutes. A fine film by Pat Ferrero about the Hopi, especially in terms of the religious symbolism of corn.

Hopi Tutu-veh-ni. 1986. Vol. 1, no. 2. Tribal publication outlines history of Big Mountain land dispute; contains many maps and commentaries by Hopis and non-Hopis.

Hough, Walter. 1918a. *The Hopi Indians: Mesa Folk of Hopiland.* Cedar Rapids, Iowa: Torch. Important firsthand account of Hopi at the turn of the century, with some reliance on Fewkes and Voth.

———. 1918b. "The Hopi Indian Collection in the United States National Museum." *Proceedings of the U.S. National Museum* 54:235–96. Good description, with pictures, of traditional Hopi material culture.

Hultkrantz, Åke. 1965. "Type of Religion in the Arctic Hunting Cultures: A Religio-Ecological Approach." In *Hunting and Fishing,* ed. Harold Hvarfner, pp. 265–318. Lulea: Norrbottens Museum. Hultkrantz is the most prolific scholar of Native American religions; works listed here deal with the relationship of religion and ecology.

———. 1966. "An Ecological Approach to Religion." *Ethnos* 31:131–50.

———. 1974. "Ecology of Religion: Its Scope and Methodology." *Review of Ethnology* 4:1–7, 9–12.

———. 1976. "Religion and Ecology among the Great Basin Indian." In *The Realm of the Extra-Human: Ideas and Actions,* ed. Agehandanda Bharati, pp. 137–50. The Hague: Mouton.

———. 1979. *The Religions of the American Indians.* Trans. Monica Setterwall. Berkeley: University of California Press.

James, Harry C. 1939. "How the Great Chief Made the Sun." *Desert* 2:22. Brief account of Hopi myth concerning the sun's origin as told to James.

———. 1974. *Pages from Hopi History.* Tucson: University of Arizona Press. Excellent historical account of the Hopi, especially from the Spanish conquest to the early twentieth century.

James, William. 1958. *The Varieties of Religious Experience*. New York: Mentor.

Jensen, Adolf. 1963. *Myth and Cult among Primitive Peoples*. Chicago: University of Chicago Press.

Jones, W. 1905. "The Algonkin Manitou." *Journal of American Folk-Lore* 18:183–90. Early description of the Fox understanding of the sacred.

Kabotie, Fred. 1977. *Fred Kabotie: Hopi Indian Artist*. Flagstaff: Museum of Northern Arizona with Northland Press. An important autobiography by a fully initiated Hopi who excels in artwork.

Kalectaca, Milo. 1978. *Lessons in Hopi*. Ed. Ronald Langacker. Tucson: University of Arizona Press. Well-organized, concise introduction to the Hopi language with a small but useful lexicon.

Katsi: Happiness, Health and Peace. 1984. Report of the Fourth Annual Hopi Mental Health Conference. Hopi Tribe Health Department. Significant presentations by a number of respected Hopis, including Percy Lomaquahu, Starlie Lomayaktewa, Radford Quamahongnewa, and Emory Sekaquaptewa; also contains a glossary of the Hopi alphabet by Sekaquaptewa.

Kavena, Juanita Tiger. 1980. *Hopi Cookery*. Tucson: University of Arizona Press. A collection of Hopi recipes with important remarks about the sacredness of Hopi foods.

Kealunohomoku, Joann W. 1980. "The Drama of the Hopi Ogres." In *Southwestern Indian Ritual Drama*, ed. Charlotte J. Frisbee, pp. 37–69. Albuquerque: University of New Mexico Press. Discusses the significance of Hopi ogre dramas, an underworked area in the literature.

Kennard, Edward A. 1937. "Hopi Reactions to Death." *American Anthropologist* 39:491–96. Discusses Hopi perceptions of death, especially as the dead are addressed in prayer.

———. 1965. "Post-War Economic Changes among the Hopi." In *Essays in Economic Anthropology*, ed. June Helm, pp. 25–32. Seattle: University of Washington Press. Describes change of Hopi economy from a subsistence base supplemented by cash to a cash base supplemented by subsistence modes.

———. 1972. "Metaphor and Magic: Key Concepts in Hopi Culture and Their Linguistic Forms." In *Studies in Linguistics*, ed. M. E. Smith, pp. 468–73. The Hague: Mouton. Discussion and interpretation of several Hopi terms related to religion.

Kitagawa, Joseph M. 1967. "Primitive, Classical, and Modern Religions: A Perspective on Understanding." In *The History of Religions: Essays on the Problem of Understanding*, ed. Joseph M. Kitagawa. Chicago: University of Chicago Press. An important typology of religious orientations by a prominent historian of religions.

Krutz, Gordon V. 1973. "The Native's Point of View as an Important Factor in Understanding the Dynamics of the Oraibi Split." *Ethnohistory* 20:77–89. Argues that the breakup of Oraibi was planned by Hopi elders; based on information given by Emory Sekaquaptewa.

Laird, David W. 1977. *Hopi Bibliography*. Tucson: University of Arizona

Press. The most comprehensive annotated Hopi bibliography, with almost 3,000 entries.

Lamphere, Louise, 1969. "Symbolic Elements in Navajo Ritual." *Southwestern Journal of Anthropology* 25:279–305. Discusses Navajo experience of the sacred.

Leach, Edmund R., ed. 1962. "Pulleyar and the Lord Buddha: An Aspect of Religous Syncretism in Ceylon." *Psychoanalysis and the Psychoanalytic View* 35:80–102. Discusses religion in terms of active mode (concerned with life) and passive mode (concerned with life after death).

———. 1968. *Dialectic in Practical Religion*. Cambridge: Cambridge University Press. Discusses the theories of "practical" (this life) and "philosophical" (next life) religion.

Leenhardt, Maurice. 1979. *Do Kamo: Person and Myth in the Melanesian World*. Trans. Basia M. Gulati. Chicago: University of Chicago Press. Explores myth and primary modes of perception among the natives of New Caledonia, New Hebrides.

Lévi-Strauss, Claude. 1966. *The Savage Mind*. Chicago: University of Chicago Press. Outlines a classification of humanity into primitive and modern categories.

Lévy-Bruhl, Lucien. 1910. *Les fonctions mentales dans les sociétés inférieures*. Paris. Argues that primitive people, unlike moderns, perceived no distance between themselves and the world.

———. 1922. *La mentalité primitive*. Paris.

Lewis, Allison. 1981. "Orientation to the Natural World: A Personal View of Ritual and Ceremony in Hopi Society." *Telescope* 1:110–18. A Hopi woman's perspective on Hopi religion, especially in the contemporary world.

Lewis, James R. 1988. "Shamans and Prophets: Continuities and Discontinuities in Native American New Religions." *American Indian Quarterly* 12:221–28. Argues for a Christian influence on a number of Native American prophets, including Wovoka and Smohalla.

Linton, Ralph, ed. 1940. *Acculturation in Seven American Indian Tribes*. New York. An important work on Native American culture contact and change; especially pertinent is Linton's distinction between "directed" (forced) and "non-directed" (peaceful) cultural change.

Loftin, John D. 1983. "Emergence and Ecology: A Religio-Ecological Interpretation of the Hopi Way." Ph.D. diss., Duke University. A synthesis of several works on the Hopi.

———. 1986. "Supplication and Participation: The Distance and Relation of the Sacred in Hopi Prayer Rites." *Anthropos* 81:177–201. Argues that Hopi prayer rites do not employ "sympathetic magic."

———. 1987. "Mythic and Historical Modes of Understanding: A Hopi-Anglo Dialogue." Unpublished manuscript. Examines Hopi and white ways of understanding reality.

Long, Charles H. 1963a. "The Meaning of Religion in the Contemporary Study of the History of Religions." *Criterion* 2:23–26. A short overview of the history of religions, ending with an argument that data and theory should be commensurate.

———. 1963b. *Alpha: The Myths of Creation.* New York: George Braziller. Classification and interpretation of a wide selection of creation mythologies.

———. 1967. "Prolegomena to a Religious Hermeneutic." *History of Religions* 6:254–64. Interprets religion as a concern for and release from the problems of society through a variety of traditions.

———. 1980. "Primitive/Civilized: The Locus of a Problem." *History of Religions* 20:43–61. Charts the history of the ideology of the "primitive," deconstructing that term.

———. 1985. "New Space, New Time: Disjunctions and Context for New World Religions." *Criterion* 24:2–7. Argues that American religious studies should be discussed in terms of New World religions, since Americans are new peoples, not unchanged remnants from Europe, Africa, and America.

Lowie, Robert H. 1922. "The Religion of the Crow Indians." In *Anthropological Papers of the American Museum of Natural History*, vol. 25, no. 2. General overview of Crow religion, including a discussion of the Crow view of the supernatural.

———. 1929a. "Notes on Hopi Clans." In *Anthropological Papers of the American Museum of Natural History*, vol. 30, pt. 6, pp. 303–60.

———. 1929b. "Hopi Kinship." In *Anthropological Papers of the American Museum of Natural History*, vol. 30, pt. 7. Important early work on Hopi social structure through a discussion of kinship.

Malotki, Ekkehart. 1978. *Hopitutuwutsi, Hopi Tales: A Bilingual Collection of Hopi Indian Stories.* Flagstaff: Museum of Northern Arizona. Myths and folktales recorded from Herschel Talashoma; includes standardized orthography by Malotki, the foremost linguistic authority on the writing of the Hopi language.

———. 1983a. "Hopiikwa Panqqawu'u. 'Say it in Hopi.' Language as a Key to Cultural Understanding." Unpublished manuscript. Examines a number of Hopi phenomena, such as warfare and kachinas, through a translation of Hopi remarks about them; argues that a knowledge of the Hopi language is essential in understanding Hopi culture.

———. 1983b. *Hopi Time: A Linguistic Analysis of the Temporal Concepts in the Hopi Language.* Berlin: Mouton. Presents more than 2,200 sentences in Hopi to disprove Whorf's claim that the Hopi have no linguistic reference to time.

Malotki, Ekkehart, and Michael Lomatuway'ma. 1987a. *Stories of Maasaw: A Hopi God.* Lincoln: University of Nebraska Press. A bilingual (Hopi-English) collection of Maasaw stories with glossary.

———. 1987b. *Maasaw: Profile of a Hopi God.* Lincoln: University of Nebraska Press. A fine ethnographic account of a complex Hopi deity; includes several bilingual texts.

Mandelbaum, David G. 1966. "Transcendental and Pragmatic Aspects of

Religion." *American Anthropologist* 78:1174–91. Classifies religion into transcendental and pragmatic concerns.

Marett, R. R. 1909. *The Threshold of Religion*. London: Methuen. Argues that religion is first expressed in dance, not in thought.

Matthews, Washington. 1888. "Legend of the Snake Order of the Moquis." *Journal of American Folk-Lore* 1:109–14. Straightforward retelling of Hopi snake myth from First Mesa.

McCluskey, Stephen C. 1979. "The Astronomy of the Hopi Indians." *Journal for the History of Astronomy* 8:174–95. Description of Hopi astronomy computed into scientific language.

Means, Florence C. 1960. *Sunlight on the Hopi Mesas: The Story of Abigail E. Johnson.* Philadelphia: Judson Press. A Baptist missionary's experience of the Hopi, 1901–37.

Miller, Horton H. 1910. Annual Report to the Superintendent of the Moqui Indian School, Keams Canyon, Arizona. In Annual Report to the Commissioner of Indian Affairs, circular no. 433. Important document for historical changes experienced by the Hopi at the turn of the twentieth century.

Mindeleff, Victor. 1891. "A Study of Pueblo Architecture: Tusayan and Cibola." Smithsonian Institution, Bureau of Ethnology, 8th Annual Report, 1886–1887, pp. 3–228. Washington: Government Printing Office. Detailed description with some interpretation of major Hopi and Zuni architectural forms.

Momaday, N. Scott. 1976. "Native American Attitudes to the Environment." In Capps 1976, pp. 79–85. A Kiowa distinguishes Native American perceptions of the environment from those of European-Americans.

Mooney, James. 1972. *Myths of the Cherokee and Sacred Formulas of the Cherokee.* Nashville: Charles Elder. A massive work on mythology and medicine, with notes and glossary.

Murdock, George P. 1941. *Ethnographic Bibliography of North America*, pp. 142–45. New Haven, Conn.: Yale University Press. One of the most complete listings of scholarly works about the Hopi; still good for works before 1940.

Nagata, Shuichi. 1970. *Modern Transformation of Moenkopi Pueblo.* Urbana: University of Illinois Press. An excellent analysis of a little-known Hopi village which explores Hopi factionalism.

Natwanaiwaia: A Hopi Philosophical Statement with George Nasoftie. 1979. New York: Clearwater. A Hopi video production featuring an elder from Shungopavi village talking about the religious meaning of farming.

Nequatewa, Edmund. 1931. "Hopi Hopiwime: The Ceremonial Calendar." *Museum Notes, Museum of Northern Arizona* 3:1–4. Brief overview of the Hopi ceremonial calendar by a fully initiated Hopi from Second Mesa who was educated in American schools.

———. 1933. "Hopi Courtship and Marriage, Second Mesa." *Museum Notes, Museum of Northern Arizona* 5:41–54. Description and interpretation of Hopi marriage and courtship customs.

————. 1940. "The Morning-Echo Days—The Old Hopi Way of Life." *Plateau* 13:15–16. Description and interpretation of ancient Hopi customs.

————. 1943. "Some Hopi Recipes for the Preparation of Wild Plant Foods." *Plateau* 16:18–20. Description of ancestral Hopi wild vegetable recipes; especially interesting for its glimpse of the Hopi hunting-gathering life.

————. 1946a. "How the Hopi Respect the Game Animals." *Plateau* 18:61–62. Hopi perceptions and understandings of wild game and hunting techniques described and interpreted.

————. 1946b. "The Place of Corn and Feathers in Hopi Ceremonies." *Plateau* 19:15–16. Brief general look at the Hopi ceremonial use of sacred cornmeal and prayer feathers.

————. 1948. "Chaveyo: The First Kachina." *Plateau* 20:60–62. Myth about the origin of Hopi kachina ceremonies.

————. 1967. *Truth of a Hopi: Stories Relating to the Origin, Myths and Clan Histories of the Hopi.* Flagstaff: Northland Press with the Museum of Northern Arizona. Fine collection of Hopi emergence and migration myths as well as some folktales told by a Hopi.

O'Kane, Walter C. 1950. *Sun in the Sky.* Norman: University of Oklahoma Press. Good introduction by a nonspecialist to Hopi life, including subsistence modes, kinship, the ceremonial calendar, and the modern situation; recommended by the late Pueblo Indian and scholar Edward Dozier.

————. 1953. *The Hopis: Portrait of a Desert People.* Norman: University of Oklahoma Press. A personal view of Hopi life that draws upon interviews with Hopi elders; nicely supplements *Sun in the Sky.*

Ortiz, Alfonzo. 1972. "Ritual Drama and the Pueblo World View." In *New Perspectives on the Pueblos,* ed. Alfonso Ortiz, pp. 135–61. Albuquerque: University of New Mexico Press. A Pueblo Indian anthropologist discusses the religious theory and practice of the Pueblo.

Otto, Rudolf. 1923. *The Idea of the Holy: An Inquiry into the Nonrational Factor in the Idea of the Divine and Its Relation to the Rational.* Trans. John W. Harvey. Oxford: Oxford University Press. Argues for the authenticity of religious experience as a constituent structure in human consciousness.

Overholt, Thomas W. 1979. "American Indians as 'Natural Ecologists.'" *American Indian Journal* 5:9–16. Argues that white Americans may learn important values concerning the proper care of the earth from Native Americans.

Page, Jake. 1982a. "Inside the Sacred Hopi Homeland." *National Georgraphic* 62:607–29.

————. 1982b. *Hopi.* New York: Harry Abrams. A nontechnical overview of contemporary Hopi life with beautiful photographs by Susanne Page; relies heavily on firsthand information from several Hopi consultants, especially Emory Koochwatewa from Shipaulovi, Second Mesa. See the supportive review of this work by Donald

Bahr and Emory Sekaquaptewa in *American Indian Quarterly*, Winter 1984, pp. 68–71.

———. 1983. "Return of the Kachinas." *Science* 4:58–63. Discusses ethical problems involved in displaying Hopi artifacts in public museums.

Parsons, Elsie Clews. 1923. "The Hopi Wowochim Ceremony in 1920." *American Anthropologist* 25:156–87. Detailed account of a First Mesa Wuwitsim rite.

———. 1924. "The Religion of the Pueblo Indians." *Proceedings of the International Congress of Americanists* 21:140–61. Outlines basic features of Pueblo religion, along with Parsons's theory of Pueblo prayer as twofold: magical control and supplication of deities.

———. 1925. *A Pueblo Indian Journal, 1919–1921.* Menasha, Wis.: American Anthropological Association. Kraus Reprint, Millwood, N.Y., 1974. Journal allegedly kept by a First Mesa Hopi named Crow-Wing, though the Hopi-Tewa Albert Yava claims in his autobiography (1978) that no Hopi by that name lived on First Mesa; perhaps Crow-Wing was a pseudonym to hide the identity of the informant.

———. 1933. *Hopi and Zuni Ceremonialism.* Menasha, Wis.: American Anthropological Association. Comparison of Hopi and Zuni religions according to topical chapters: curing and weather control, society and clan, kachina, use of kivas, hierarchy, calendar, values, pantheon, etc.; also relates Hopi clan origin myths.

———. 1939. *Pueblo Indian Religion.* 2 vols. Chicago: University of Chicago Press. An excellent source book; the introduction includes a few theoretical considerations of interest to scholars.

Peterson, Charles H. 1971. "The Hopis and the Mormons—1858–1873." *Utah Historical Quarterly* 39:179–94. History of early Mormon-Hopi contacts, with evidence for the presence of Hopi prophecies about the arrival of whites.

Powell, John Wesley. 1972. *The Hopi Villages: The Ancient Province of Tusayan.* Palmer Lake, Colo.: Filter Press, 1972. Originally published in *Scribner's Monthly* 11:193–213. A detailed description of Hopi by a good friend of the Hopi and excellent observer.

Qoyawayma, Polingaysi. 1964. *No Turning Back: A True Account of a Hopi Girl's Struggle to Bridge the Gap between the World of Her People and the World of the White Man.* Albuquerque: University of New Mexico Press. Autobiography of Elizabeth White (Polingaysi Qoyawayma), a Hopi who became a teacher in order to help Hopi children make an easier transition to the dominant society; though White converted to Christianity as a young girl and that perhaps colors a number of her understandings, the book helps illuminate the problems faced by Hopis in the early twentieth century.

Qua'Töqti: The Eagle's Call. Hopi Publishers, Kykotsmovi, Ariz. A privately owned and operated weekly newspaper edited by former tribal chairman Abbot Sekaquaptewa; an excellent primary source for contemporary Hopi Reservation events and Hopi perspectives on important issues.

Rappaport, Roy. 1979. *Ecology, Meaning and Religion*. Richmond, Calif.: North Atlantic Books.

Sahlins, Marshall. 1972. *Stone Age Economics*. New York: Aldine. Essay collection revealing the religious dimension of primitive economics.

Schlegel, Alice. 1977. "Male and Female in Hopi Thought and Action." In *Sexual Stratification: A Cultural View*, ed. A. Schlegel, pp. 245–69. New York: Columbia University Press. Fills a major gap in the literature by outlining Hopi female modalities on several planes of significance.

Sekakuku, Chief Joe. 1939. "When the Hopi Deserted Their Ancient Gods." *Desert* 3:16–18. Recounts the Hopi legend of the destruction of Awatobi village, with insights by a twentieth-century Hopi concerning his involvement in the dominant culture.

Sekaquaptewa, Emory. 1972. "Preserving the Good Things of Hopi Life." In *Plural Society in the Southwest*, ed. E. H. Spicer and R. H. Thompson, pp. 239–60. New York: Weatherhead Foundation, Interbook. An historical overview of the split of Oraibi and the settlement of Hotevilla as well as Hopi legal disputes over land holdings with the U.S. government and the Navajo; suggests a mode by which the Hopi may maintain their traditional values while dealing fruitfully with the dominant culture. Sekaquaptewa is a Third Mesa Hopi involved in Hopi ceremonialism and is also coordinator of Indian Programs at the University of Arizona at Tucson.

———. 1976. "Hopi Indian Ceremonies." In Capps 1976, pp. 35–43. Discusses Hopi kachina initiation and some basic Hopi religious perceptions.

———. 1979. "One More Smile for a Hopi Clown." *Parabola* 4:6–9. Detailed description and interpretation of Hopi clowning.

———. 1980a. "The Hopi Tricentennial Year and Era." *Qua'Töqti*, Aug. 7, 1980, pp. 1 and 3. Brief overview of the Pueblo Revolt that overturned Spanish rule, with interesting comments about current Hopi perceptions of the relation between individuals and society.

———. 1980b. Prologue. In Washburn 1980. Interprets a Hopi prophecy to mean that education will help the Hopi deal more effectively with the culture of the white man.

———. 1980c. Glossary of the Hopi Alphabet. In Washburn 1980. A nontechnical alphabet of the Hopi language that is commonly used by native speakers.

———. 1984. "Hopi Language." In *Katsi: Happiness, Health and Peace* 1984, pp. 96–98. Bilingual text about the importance of the Hopi language to the Hopi people.

Sekaquaptewa, Emory, and Kathleen M. Sands. 1978. "Four Hopi Lullabies: A Study in Method and Meaning." *American Indian Quarterly* 4:195–210. Translates and transliterates four Hopi songs, placing them in their broad Hopi cultural context.

Sekaquaptewa, Helen. 1969. *Me and Mine: The Life Story of Helen Sekaquaptewa as Told to Louise Udall*. Tucson: University of Arizona Press.

Autobiography of a Hopi woman that provides much data about the Hopi way during the first half of the twentieth century.

Shorris, Earl. 1971. *The Death of the Great Spirit.* New York: New American Library. Contains interviews with Emory Sekaquaptewa and Peter Nuvamsa.

Smith, Jonathan Z. 1971–72. "I Am a Parrot (Red)." *History of Religions* 11:391–413. Provocative reinterpretation of the literature concerning Bororos' statements that they are parrots.

Spicer, Edward H. 1954. "Spanish-Indian Acculturation in the Southwest." *American Anthropologist* 56:663–84. A seminal paper that introduced the concept that "compartmentalization" was one response of Rio Grande Pueblos to white dominance.

————, ed. 1971. *Perspectives in American Indian Culture Change.* Chicago: University of Chicago Press. Essays by Spicer, Edward P. Dozier, Edward M. Bruner, Evon Z. Vogt, David French, and Helen Codere. Spicer outlines four basic types of culture change—incorporation, compartmentalization, fusion, and assimilation.

Stephen, Alexander M. 1898. "Pigments in Ceremonials of the Hopi." *International Folk-Lore Association Archives* 1:260–65. Discusses the use of colors as prayers for rain from the cardinal directions.

————. 1929. "Hopi Tales." *Journal of American Folk-Lore* 42:1–72. Important collection of Hopi emergence and migration myths and folktales.

————. 1936. *Hopi Journal.* Ed. Elsie C. Parsons, with an additional glossary by Benjamin L. Whorf. New York: Columbia University Press. An invaluable source of data from First Mesa, still used extensively as a primary reference by scholars. Stephen spent many years with the Hopi from the late nineteenth to the early twentieth century and acquired the trust of several elders. I have heard some Hopis say, however, that although Stephen's drawings are accurate his interpretations of them are not, because his consultants deliberately misled him once they realized his intention to publish.

————. 1939–40. "Hopi Indians of Arizona." *Masterkey* 13, no. 6, and 14, nos. 1 and 3–6. Overview of Hopi life and religion with emphasis on the snake dance.

Steward, Julian H. 1931. "Notes on Hopi Ceremonies in Their Initiatory Form in 1927–1928." *American Anthropologist* 33:56–79. Detailed descriptions of Wuwtsim, Soyalangw, and Powamuya.

————. 1938. "Basin-Plateau Aboriginal Socio-Political Groups." *Smithsonian Institution, Bureau of American Ethnology, Bulletin 120.* Definitive work on Great Basin hunter-gatherer societies—prehistoric Hopi ancestors.

Stewart, Guy R., and Ernest A. Nicholson. 1940. "Water Conservation in Hopi Agriculture." *Soil Conservation* 6:45–48 and 51. Description of Hopi horticultural practices and an analysis of how they conserve water.

Talayesva, Don. 1942. *Sun Chief: The Autobiography of a Hopi Indian.* New Haven, Conn.: Yale University Press. Perhaps the finest, most insightful autobiography by a fully initiated Hopi; presents a detailed picture of Hopi life, including problems facing the twentieth-century Hopi, without violating ceremonial secrets and customs.

Thompson, Laura, and Alice Joseph. 1944. *The Hopi Way*. Lawrence, Kans.: Haskell Institute for the U.S. Indian Service. Good introduction to the traditional Hopi way; includes results of psychological tests administered to Hopi children.

Titiev, Mischa. 1938. "Dates of Planting at the Hopi Indian Pueblo of Oraibi." *Museum Notes, Museum of Northern Arizona* 11:39–42. Delineates the traditional planting times at Oraibi as determined by points on the eastern horizon above which the sun rises in spring and summer.

————. 1944a. *Old Oraibi: A Study of the Hopi Indians of Third Mesa*. Cambridge, Mass.: Peabody Museum. An excellent detailed overview of Third Mesa life by a foremost authority on Hopi culture; includes discussions of subsistence modes, kinship structures, and ceremonies. Both a synthesis of old studies and a collection of data gained in the field, this work remains invaluable, though Titiev's social structural view of Hopi religion and his interpretation of Hopi prayer as magical are controversial.

————. 1944b. "Two Hopi Tales from Oraibi." *Michigan Academy of Science, Arts and Letters Papers* 29:425–37. "The Stolen Spring" and "Sitiyo and the Hawk," with helpful notes.

Toelken, Barre. 1976. "How Many Sheep Will It Hold?" In Capps 1976, pp. 9–24. Insightful study of Native American perception; includes material on the Hopi.

United States District Court. 1962. *Opinion of the Court, Healing v. Jones*. San Francisco: Pernau-Walsh. An important Native American land claims case in which the Hopi sued the Navajo to gain control of the entire reservation as established by President Arthur in 1882. The court found that the Hopi should have complete ownership of District 6 and that the remainder of the land should be shared, though it did not specify details.

Van der Leeuw, G. 1963. *Sacred and Profane Beauty: The Holy in Art*. Trans. David E. Green. New York: Holt, Rinehart & Winston. A study of religious symbolism in art that includes interesting methological considerations.

Vecsey, Christopher. 1980. "American Indian Environmental Religions." In *American Indian Environments: Ecological Issues in Native American History*, ed. Christopher Vecsey and Robert W. Venable, pp. 1–37. Syracuse, N.Y.: Syracuse University Press. Explores the relationship between religion and ecology among Native Americans.

————. 1988. Review of Sam D. Gill's *Mother Earth*. *American Indian Quarterly* 12:254–56.

Voth, Henry R. N.d. Interview with Yukioma. In Mennonite Library and Archives, Bethel College, North Newton, Kans. Sheds light on early twentieth-century Hopi perceptions of white Americans.

————. 1901. *The Oraibi Powamu Ceremony*. Chicago: Field Columbian

Museum. A detailed description by a Mennonite missionary to Hopi who was an excellent observer of Hopi life and spoke fluent Hopi; much of his information, while accurate, was obtained in a rather unethical manner, usually by forcing his way into situations in which he was considered off limits by the Hopi.

———. 1905a. *Oraibi Natal Customs and Ceremonies*, pp. 43–61. Chicago: Field Columbian Museum. Good detailed description.

———. 1905b. *The Traditions of the Hopi*. Chicago: Field Columbian Museum. Important source of Hopi oral traditions that gives names and villages of informants.

———. 1912. *Brief Miscellaneous Hopi Papers*, pp. 89–149. Chicago: Field Columbian Museum.

———. 1915. *Hopi Proper Names*, pp. 63–113. Chicago: Field Columbian Museum. Detailed listing of Hopi names with translations.

———. 1967. *The Henry R. Voth Hopi Indian Collection at Grand Canyon, Arizona*. Phoenix: Byron Harvey. Important collection of Hopi material culture.

Wach, Joachim. 1951. *Types of Religious Experience*. Chicago: University of Chicago Press. Essay collection by a historian of religions; especially valuable for its theoretical considerations.

Wallis, Wilson D. 1936. "Folk Tales from Shumopovi, Second Mesa." *Journal of American Folk-Lore* 49:1–68. Good collection of oral traditions; still useful as a primary source.

Wallis, Wilson D., and Mischa Titiev. 1944. "Hopi Notes from Chimopovy." *Michigan Academy of Science, Arts and Letters Papers* 30:523–56. With 20 plates. Notes recorded by Wallis from a 1912 interview with Joshua Humiyesva, a resident of Shongopavi. Topics discussed are food, material culture, rites of passage, witchcraft, and war. Humiyesva's comments are compared with some found in Titiev's fieldwork from the 1930s.

Washburn, Dorothy K., ed. 1980. *Hopi Kachina: Spirit of Life*. Seattle: California Academy of Science and the University of Washington Press. Important collection of essays by E. Charles Adams and Deborah Hull, Watson Smith, Washburn, John Connelly, Clara and John Tanner, and J. J. Brody, with a prologue and glossary of the Hopi alphabet by Emory Sekaquaptewa and an introduction by Washburn; well received by the Hopi.

Waters, Frank. 1963. *Book of the Hopi*. New York: Ballantine. This book, while widely read and accepted, may not be reliable. Emory Sekaquaptewa told me that much of the information is inaccurate and that several ceremonial secrets as well as informants' names were improperly published. For another Hopi criticism, see Yava 1978, p. 81. For a detailed critique, see Armin W. Geertz, "Book of the Hopi: The Hopis' Book," *Anthropos* 78 (1983) :547–56.

Whiteley, Peter M. 1982. "Third Mesa Hopi Social Structural Dynamics and Socio-cultural Change: The View from Bacavi." Ph.D. diss., University of New Mexico. A three-volume history of Third Mesa using extensive historical documents and Hopi consultants.

——. 1983. "The Meaning of the Oraibi Split: Hopi Explanation and Anthropological Interpretation." Unpublished manuscript. A condensed version of twentieth-century culture change at Third Mesa based on Whiteley's doctoral dissertation.

——. 1985. "Unpacking Hopi 'Clans': Another Vintage Model out of Africa?" *Journal of Anthropological Research* 41:357–74. Argues that Hopi clanship's significance is primarily mythological and ritual—a significant development in Hopi studies, though Whiteley perhaps overstates the tension between his view and social structural perspectives.

——. 1986. "Unpacking Hopi 'Clans': Another Vintage Model out of Africa?" *Journal of Anthropological Research* 42:69–79. Second part of the preceding paper.

——. 1988a. *Deliberate Acts: Changing Hopi Culture through the Oraibi Split.* Tucson: University of Arizona Press. An important ethnohistorical account of the 1906 split of Oraibi village.

——. 1988b. *Bacavi: Journey to Red Springs.* Flagstaff, Ariz.: Northland Press. A more popular analysis of Bacavi than the one given in *Deliberate Acts;* filled with excellent late nineteenth and early twentieth-century photographs of Third Mesa. Foreword by Hopi Leigh Jenkins Honheptewa.

Whiting, Alfred F. 1939. "Ethnobotany of the Hopi." *Museum of Northern Arizona Bulletin 15.* Primary source identifying plants in the Hopi environment and telling how the Hopi use them.

Whitson, Hollis A. 1985. "A Policy Review of the Federal Government's Relocation of Navajo Indians under P.L. 93-531 and P.L. 96-305." *Arizona Law Review* 27:372–414. Detailed examination of the Hopi-Navajo land dispute, well researched and a source of many data, though Whitson obviously supports the Navajo and Hopi traditionalists.

Whorf, Benjamin L. 1950. "An American Indian Model of the Universe," ed. Edward Kennard. *International Journal of American Linguistics* 16:67–72. Overview of Hopi concept of time as a process of becoming later and later; argues that the Hopi have no real concept of time as historical duration, a theory Malotki 1983b repudiates. This essay was reprinted in John B. Carroll, ed., *Language, Thought, and Reality: Selected Writings of Benjamin Lee Whorf,* Cambridge, Mass.: MIT Press, 1956, pp. 57–64.

Wilson, Maggie. 1980. "The Hopi Today: A Nation in Transition." *Arizona Highways* 56:29–42. A good source of comments by several Hopis about the current Hopi orientation to the world.

Wright, Barton. 1973. *Kachinas: A Hopi Artist's Documentary.* Original paintings by Cliff Bahnimptewa. Flagstaff, Ariz.: Northland Press. Interprets (sometimes critically) 237 paintings of Hopi kachinas by Moencopi resident Clifford Bahnimptewa; also gives the season or time when the kachinas appear as well as their particular function and meaning.

——. 1977. *Hopi Kachinas: The Complete Guide to Collecting Kachina Dolls.*

Flagstaff, Ariz: Northland Press. Describes and interprets a number of kachina dolls.

——. 1979. *Hopi Material Culture: Artifacts Gathered by H. R. Voth in the Fred Harvey Collection.* With an introduction by Byron Harvey III and an essay on Voth's ethnology by Fred Eggan. Flagstaff, Ariz.: Northland Press and Heard Museum. Covers dress, tools and devices, and ritual objects.

Yava, Albert. 1978. *Big Falling Snow: A Tewa-Hopi Indian's Life and Times and the History and Traditions of His People.* Ed. Harold Courlander. New York: Crown. Presents important information about the Hopi way and should be read by all serious students of Hopi; represents a First Mesa viewpoint that can be compared with the Second Mesa perspective of Kabotie 1977 and the Third Mesa standpoint of Talayesva 1942.

Younger, Erin, and Victor Masayesva, Jr. 1983. *Hopi Photographers/Hopi Images.* Tucson: Sun Tracks and the University of Arizona Press. Includes a history of photography of the Hopi, contemporary photographs and poems about Hopi by Hopi, and a valuable introduction to the Hopi understanding of photography by Masayesva.

Index of Hopi Terms

*Emory Sekaquaptewa (personal communication, 1990) has stated that *navoti* is best translated "tradition" or "knowledge" rather than "prophecy." For him, "prophecy" implies fatalism, whereas *navoti* refers to traditions which foretell the consequences of improper living. It should be understood that Hopis are not predestined to act improperly so as to bring about their prophecies.

Subject and Name Index

chief of all clouds, 42, 43, 44; as
Tcowilawu, 48
God of Death (Maasaw): 127n.25,
135n.37; Owner of Hopiland, 9–11;
taught farming, 11–12; gave fire,
23, 76; mining, 94
God of High Winds: 44–45
Good heart: 34; necessary for life, 77–
78
Great Basin Shoshoni: relation to
Hopi, 23, 104

Hamblin, Jacob: 68
Hawk (Kiisa): taught Hopi how to
hunt, 23; male sacrality, 23, 26
Home Dance: 43, 92
Hopi: 110
Hopi Constitution: 86; problem of de-
fining tribal member, 104–105; elec-
tions, 106–107
Hopi Cultural Center: 101
Hopi Health Manpower Development
Program: 108
Hopi Land Operations Office: 110
Hopi Law: 112; blue corn, 5
Hopi logic: as practical, 19–20, 42, 43
Hopi reservation: 72
Hopi Tribal Council: 106, 120, 121; be-
ginning, 82; resulted in Hopi fac-
tions, 82–83; forced response to
dominance, 84
Hotevilla: 33, 34, 35, 75, 98, 102,
136n.48
Houses: 87–88
Hunting: clans, 22–24; male activity,
24–28

Indian Health Service: 108
Initiation: Kachina, 20, 34, 46, 49–51;
Wuwtsim, 26, 31, 35, 56, 79,
130n.73; Powamuy, 34, 46–48

Kachina: Crow-wing, 20, 50; clan, 20;
return, 21; Owl, 23, 112; (Ewtoto)
chief, 45; Ahooli, 45; Patsavu Hu',
46; Mudhead, 50, 133n.50; Whippers, 50, 56, 112; Giant, 53; Hahay'i
Wuuti (Mother), 53, 54; Hee'e'e
(Mother), 56; ceremonies, 57; spinach, 105; Santa Claus, 107,
141n.96; discussion, 133n.38; departure of real kachinas, 134n.63
Kachina chief: 39–54 passim

Kawestima: 78, 136n.48
Keams, Thomas: 70, 72
Kewanimptewa: 79
Kikotsmovi village: 33, 111

La Farge, Oliver: 82
Land: problems with Navajos and
whites, 89–92; coal mining, 93–96;
religion, 119; importance, 138n.24
Lawshe, Abraham: 80
Lololoma: 72, 73, 75, 136n.51
Lomahongyoma: 73, 74

Medicine water: 41
Men: 20–28; like hawks, 26; control
ceremonies, 27; link with corn and
hawks, 30–32
Mishongnovi: 94, 109
Mormon: 68–69
myth: xx

Nature: as spiritual, 14
Navajo: 66, 67, 72, 74
New Year: 33

Oraibi village: 33, 57, 68, 69, 73; traditional planting times, 6; split, 75–79

Paiute: 66, 104
Phratry: 18–24; classification of na-
ture, 18–19; Hopi logic, 19; relation
to prayer and ceremony, 20–24;
Third Mesa, 20; relation to hunting
and farming, 20–24
Pima: 66
Polacca: 103
Powamuy chief: 21, 38–54 passim
Powell, John Wesley: 69–70
Prayer: 36, 40; songs, 44–45; ritual
planning, 45
Prayer stick: 37, 38
Primitive: 67, 71
Prophecy: xx, 78, 100, 113–18, 122–
23; paradox, 67, 68, 71; factional,
75; return to Oraibi to restore cere-
monies, 136n.55; Anglo education,
138n.4
Purification day: 68, 135n.4
Purification rite: 51, 52

Rain tobacco: 38
Rites of passage: birth, 28–30
Ritual: xvii–xix, 28

John D. Loftin is a visiting professor of religious studies
at the University of North Carolina, Chapel Hill.

DATE DUE

MCK RT	DEC 0 2 2003		